Drawn Away

What the Bible Actually Says About Temptation

Gage Coldwater

Deliberate Path Press

Contents

Chapter 1

The June Bug Doesn't Mean to Die

The porch light came on at dusk, and the bug zapper started humming a few minutes after. You could hear it from the kitchen if the back door was open, that low electric drone running steady as a refrigerator. Out on the porch, the blue glow lit up the underside of the eaves and threw a square of cold light across the warped boards. The bugs found it the way they always find it. The small ones came first, mostly gnats and a few of those little brown beetles that smell like dirt when you crush them. The bigger insects worked their way in after that. And eventually, the June bugs started coming.

The first one came in heavy and clumsy, the way they always do. He had a body about the size of a marble, with a hard, glossy shell the color of wet tobacco, and he droned like a little engine somebody had not tuned right. He didn't fly straight at the light because June bugs do not fly straight at anything. He came in fast and overshot the zapper, swung wide, and came back. He hit the side of the eaves and bounced. He hit a porch board and rolled over and lay there flailing his legs in the air for a few seconds before he got himself right side up and went up again. He was drawn back to the light every time he fell. Twenty minutes earlier, he had been somewhere else doing something else, climbing in the grass or looking for a mate or doing whatever a June bug does when the sun goes down. Now he was not doing any of that. He was bouncing off a square of blue light bolted to the side of a house in the middle of nowhere, and he could not, for the life of him, stop.

I watched him from the porch swing. I knew how this story ended, because I had watched it end the same way every summer that I could remember. He would crash, and he would crawl, and he would haul himself back up onto a porch board and take off again as if he had a string tied to him, drawn back to the light no matter how many times the light knocked him down. Sooner or later, his hard, glossy back would touch the wire where it should not, and there would be a sound like a firecracker dropped in dry leaves, and the June bug would drop. Sometimes he was still kicking when he landed, and sometimes he was already done.

He didn't mean to die.

That is the whole point. He had not crawled out of the grass that evening with a death wish in his chunky little head. He was not suicidal, and he was not stupid. He was a June bug doing what June bugs do, and what June bugs do every summer night of their short lives is fly toward the brightest light they can find. Something inside him was wired toward brightness. The zapper just took something normal, something he was made to do, and used it against him. By the time he understood what was happening, if he ever did, he was already too close to pull out of the spin.

That June bug is the picture of the process of temptation.

How Sin Works

This is exactly how sin works, and it has always worked this way. From the Garden of Eden to the screen in your hand, the pattern has not changed. Something looks bright, and something pulls, and a few loose laps follow, each one closer than the one before. Then comes the contact, and the sound, and the body on the boards.

You did not mean to either.

Most people think sin is mostly about the moment, the big one, the decision they regret. They think that if they could just be a little stronger when the moment came, a little tougher and a little more disciplined right at the end, they would not fall. So they brace themselves for the moment. They white-knuckle it. They make promises about what they will do next time, and next time comes, and the moment hits, and they fall again the same way they fell before, and they walk away wondering what is wrong with them.

The problem is that the moment is not where sin happens. The moment is when it finishes.

The June bug did not die at the zapper. He died on the third pass.

The Bible has known this for two thousand years. James, the half-brother of the Lord, wrote it down in plain words at the start of his letter. He did not write it for theologians. He wrote it for ordinary people scattered across the Roman world who were getting hammered by life and their own desires, and were trying to figure out how to live faithfully in the middle of it. The text is short, direct, and pulls the curtain back for us to understand better.

Read it slowly. Please read it twice if you need to.

> *"Let no man say when he is tempted, I am tempted of God: for God cannot be tempted with evil, neither tempteth he any man: But every man is tempted, when he is drawn away of his own lust, and enticed. Then when lust hath conceived, it bringeth forth sin: and sin, when it is finished, bringeth forth death."*(James 1:13-15)

That is the whole anatomy of how a person ends up doing what he swore he would never do, written out in three short verses.

Notice what James does. He does not just say, *"Don't sin."* A child can say that, and your mother said it to you before you could read. James does something more useful. He tells you how sin actually works. He hands you the wiring diagram. He says that if you want to stop dying on the porch, you have to understand what is pulling you there in the first place.

There are six major concepts found in those three verses; they are six stops on a road that ends with a body on the boards. We are going to walk through every one of them in the chapters ahead, slowly, with the text open. Before we take the road apart, look at it as a whole.

Stop One: The Source

> *"Let no man say when he is tempted, I am tempted of God: for God cannot be tempted with evil, neither tempteth he any man."* (James 1:13)

The first thing James does is rip the favorite excuse out of your hand before you can use it.

The temptation that pulled at you yesterday did not come from God. He did not drop it in your lap to see what you would do, nor did He let it loose on you to teach you a lesson. He did not arrange the situation, lay the bait, and step back to watch.

James is so emphatic about this that he doubles down. God cannot be tempted with evil. Evil holds no pull on Him at all. Because of that, He never turns around and uses evil to pull on anyone else. The bait was not His.

You will be amazed at how often, when you sit down and listen to people talk about their sin, they manage to make God a quiet partner in it. *"Well, He put me in that situation." "He knew I was going to be there." "He gave me these feelings." "He let it happen."* The implication, never quite said out loud, is that some part of the responsibility leaks back onto Him.

It does not.

We will spend the next chapter on this, because nothing else holds until you own it. As long as you can quietly pin even a sliver of the blame on God, you have an exit ramp from your own repentance. James closes that ramp on the very first verse.

Stop Two: The Pull

> *"But every man is tempted, when he is drawn away..."* (James 1:14a)

The phrase *"drawn away"* is two words in English that carry one word in Greek, *exelkomenos.* It means dragged, lured, or hauled out. It is the kind of word a fisherman or a hunter would use. You drag a fish out of its hiding place under the bank. You lure a deer out of the brush with a feeder. You pull a thing out of where it was supposed to be and into the open, where it is exposed.

Temptation pulls, and it always pulls in a direction. It pulls you out of where you were and toward where it wants you.The June bug had been on a stalk of grass a minute earlier, and the pull moved him. He turned his head, took off, and the drag had begun.

The pull is rarely violent at the start. The June bug is not yanked toward the light. He is invited by what he perceives as something good for him. The light stays on, the hum just stays steady, and he drifts toward it.

You will know the pull when you see it. The notification lights your screen, and you turn your head. A thought arrives in your head while you are trying to fall asleep, and you do not throw it back out. The conversation turns slightly off-color, and you do not turn it back. The girl walks by, the comment lands wrong, and the link sits there waiting to be clicked. Something turns your head. Something pulls.

We will spend a chapter on this, because most Christians lose the battle right here and never even know they were in one.

Stop Three: The Bait

> *"...of his own lust, and enticed."* (James 1:14b)

The Greek for *enticed* is *deleazomenos*. It comes from the same fishing world as the last word, and it means baited, like a trap baited with food or a hook baited with a worm.

But notice carefully where James locates the source. He does not say the devil baits you. He says you are drawn away of your *own* lust, and *enticed*. The pull is from inside you. The bait works because something inside you wants it.

Satan is real, and the Bible never lets you pretend otherwise. He is called the tempter (Matthew 4:3) and a roaring lion seeking whom he may devour (1 Peter 5:8). But Satan is not God. He is not everywhere at once, nor is he omniscient. He cannot be on every porch on every summer night personally tuning the wattage of every zapper to every individual bug. He is a creature, not a Creator, and he has limits. He does not know you the way God knows you, and he is not standing over your shoulder, hand-crafting a custom hook with your name etched into the shank.

The bait does not need him to be everywhere, because the bait is already loose in the world.

People put it there. Industries put it there. A whole fallen creation puts it there. Somebody decided years ago that a particular shade of red would make a person click. Somebody decided what a beer commercial should look like. Somebody decided how short the dress would be on the cover of the magazine at the gas station. Somebody wrote the algorithm that decides what shows up next on your feed. None of those people had to be Satan, and most of them were not even thinking about you in particular. They put bait into the world for money, attention, and power, and the bait floats downstream until it lands near you.

What makes that particular piece of bait work on you and not on the man next to you is not that Satan custom-built it for you. It is your own lust, your own internal pull toward that particular thing. The bait is in the water. The lust is yours.

This actually makes the picture more honest, not less. It would almost be flattering, in a twisted way, to think the Devil himself was personally crafting your downfall, because it would let you off the hook a little. *"I never had a chance.*

Satan made it just for me." But that is not what James says. James says the lust was yours, the pull was yours, and the bait worked because of what was already in you.

The boy who has no interest in alcohol but cannot put down his phone has a reason inside him. The girl who is bored by the party scene but is undone by what a certain boy says in her DMs has a reason inside her. The young man who has the discipline of a marine in every other area of his life but cannot control his temper at home has a reason inside him.

The bait does not know your name. Your lust does.

We will spend a chapter on this, because the bait you cannot stop running into in this fallen world will keep on landing near you, whether you like it or not. The real question is what is alive in you when it lands.

Stop Four: The Conception

> *"Then when lust hath conceived..."* (James 1:15a)

Now we are inside.

The pull and the bait happen out where you can see them, but the conception happens in the dark. It is the moment you stop resisting and start agreeing. It is the moment you go from *I shouldn't* to *I want to*. It is the moment the line between *being tempted* and *intending to sin* gets crossed.

Nobody around you can see it happen.

You do not need to do anything for the conception to happen. You do not need to type a word, unlock the screen, or say it out loud. You just have to nod inside your own head. You just have to give the bait a yes.

This is why Jesus said adultery happens before the act.

"Whosoever looketh on a woman to lust after her hath committed adultery with her already in his heart"(Matthew 5:28).

The act is downstream, and the conception is upstream. By the time the world sees the act, God has already seen the agreement.

This is the most important stop on the road for most people, because it is the line you can defend even after the pull has hit and even after the bait has landed. You felt the pull, but that is not your sin. You saw the bait, but that is not your sin. The moment you nodded, however, sin was conceived in you.

We have a chapter on this one too. Get this stop right, and you save yourself from most of what comes after it.

Stop Five: The Birth

> *"...it bringeth forth sin..."* (James 1:15b)

Now it is outside again. Now it is in the world. Now it is a thing you did, not just a thing you wanted.

The hand moves, the mouth opens, the screen unlocks, and the act happens. This is the moment of contact with the bug zapper for the June bug, the pop, and the smell.

This is what most people mean when they say "sin." This is what most people picture when they think about repenting. This is the visible part, the part somebody else can catch you in, the part you confess.

But it is fifth on the road. It is not first. By the time the act is born, four other things have already happened, and unless you go back and address them, you will be in the same spot again next week.

We will give this stop its chapter, because part of beating sin is being honest about how ugly the act actually is when you stop letting the bait dress it up.

Stop Six: The Finish

"...and sin, when it is finished, bringeth forth death." (James 1:15c)

This is the stop the June bug never thought about, because the June bug could not think. But you can. James says sin grows and matures, and when it reaches maturity, it gives birth to death.

That is not a metaphor. That is a wage. *"For the wages of sin is death"* (Romans 6:23). That is a harvest. *"Whatsoever a man soweth, that shall he also reap"* (Galatians 6:7). That is a real, costly, sometimes lifelong consequence that the bait did not advertise on the front of the box.

The bait never advertises the finish. The light never tells the June bug about the body on the boards. The screen never tells the boy that he will not be able to enjoy his wife in 15 years because of what is being formed in him tonight. The party never tells the girl about the relationship that she will not be able to trust because of what she gave away last weekend. The bottle never tells the young man about the children who will not know him.

But the finish is real, and it comes for every sin that runs its full course. Some of it shows up this week, some of it shows up in twenty years, and some of it does not show up until the day you stand before the Lord. But it is coming. Sin always pays. It pays late, but it pays.

We will give this stop a chapter, too, not to scare you, but to respect you enough to tell you the truth.

That is the road.

Source, pull, bait, conception, birth, death. Six stops in one direction, played out a million times a day across the world, and probably played out in your own life this week.

You have watched this happen, maybe in your own life and maybe in somebody you love.

Take the kid in your youth group who swore he would never drink. He did not go from sober to drunk in one motion. He got drawn away. Somebody texted him, somebody invited him, and somebody promised it would be chill. That was the bait. He thought about it for a week, and that was the conception. He went, and that was the birth. Whatever came after, the call from the cops, the conversation with his parents, the look on his elder's face the next Sunday, that was the finish.

Take the girl you grew up with who walked away from her purity. She did not fall in five minutes either. There were follows and likes on social media, text messages, and late-night conversations she did not tell anybody about. There was a slow circle around the zapper that she did not want to admit she was making. And then one night, the circle got too tight.

Or look closer. Look at your phone right now.

You do not even have to make this hypothetical. Pick it up, open it, and look at the apps on your phone. Look at the notifications, and look at the recommended videos. Somebody who has never met you has spent millions of dollars and thousands of hours figuring out exactly what color, exactly what sound, exactly what flash of skin, and exactly what flash of rage will make you turn your head. That little glowing rectangle in your hand is the most sophisticated bug zapper in the history of the world. It is humming, right now, in your pocket. And you have circled it tonight already. You know you have.

You did not mean to.

Application:

Here is what I want you to take from this first chapter, before we get to any of the others.

The June bug did not mean to die. The June bug is not stupid. The June bug is wired. Until somebody pulls the June bug aside and explains what light is doing to him, he will keep circling the light every summer night until he lands on the zapper.

Know this: You are not stupid either. You have been told a thousand times to *"just say no,"* but it has not worked, has it? Not really, not consistently, and not for the sin that actually has its hooks in you. You have white-knuckled your way through Sunday and crashed by Tuesday more times than you want to count. You have made promises in the parking lot after worship services and broken them before you even got home.

The reason it does not work is not that you are uniquely weak. It is because you have been trying to win a fight at stop four when the battle was already lost at stop two.

I propose that we back up at this point.

We are going to walk down this road together, slowly, with the Bible open, and we are going to look at every stop. We will learn how to spot the pull when it first starts pulling. We will learn how to recognize the bait that finds you in the world. We will learn how to deal with the lust inside you that makes the bait work. We will learn how to decide ahead of time, before the moment, what we will and will not do. And we will learn what God has promised the man and the woman who is willing to take all of this seriously.

The June bug is doomed because it has no Bible to guide it and thus, it has no hope.

You do!

Discussion Questions:

1. James says plainly that God does not tempt anyone (James 1:13). Have you ever blamed God, even quietly, for a temptation in your life? Why does that excuse have to die before any real progress can begin?

2. The author claims sin is rarely lost in the moment. It is lost on "the third pass" before the moment. Where in your own life can you see the slow circling that came before a fall?

3. Name your zapper. What is the specific temptation your own lust keeps reaching for? Be honest. You cannot fight what you will not name.

4. Reread James 1:13-15 slowly. Which of the six stops (source, pull, bait, conception, birth, death) do you think you understand the least? Which one do you think you fall on most often?

5. Why does the author compare your phone to "the most sophisticated bug zapper in the history of the world"? Do you agree? What evidence do you see in your own week?

6. What is one thing you want God to settle in you by the time you finish this book?

Chapter 2

Don't Blame God

The first time a human being ever tried to blame God for his sin, he was standing naked behind a tree. It was the cool of the day. The garden was the only place that had ever existed for him, and it had been good every minute he had been alive in it. The grass under his feet was thick and damp. The fruit on the trees hung low enough to reach without stretching. The animals he had named the day before were grazing somewhere off in the brush. A river ran out of the middle of the place in four directions and watered everything green for as far as the man could walk.

But something had changed since the morning. Something inside him had broken, and now something around him was different, too.

He heard the voice first. He had heard it every evening of his short life, and it had always been the most welcome sound in the world. The Lord God walking in the garden in the cool of the day, the footsteps among the leaves, the quiet calling of his name. Always before, the man had run toward that voice the way a child runs toward his father at the end of a long afternoon. But this evening was unlike the others. This evening, when he heard God's voice, the man crouched behind a tree with his wife, held very still, and tried to shrink.

"Adam, where art thou?"

The man's chest must have hammered within him. He could feel the bark of the tree pressing into his back. He could feel the leaves he and his wife had stitched together that afternoon scratching at his skin. He could feel something cold and thick in his stomach that he had never felt before. It would be a long time before anyone gave it a name. Eventually, they would call it shame.

He answered from behind the tree.

"I heard thy voice in the garden, and I was afraid, because I was naked; and I hid myself."

God already knew. God had known before God called. The question was not for the information. The question was intended to make the man answer it. So the man would have to step out from behind the tree. So the man would have to look his actions in the face and say what he had done.

"Who told thee that thou wast naked? Hast thou eaten of the tree, whereof I commanded thee that thou shouldest not eat?"

Here is where it happened. Here is where, for the first time in human history, a man caught in his own sin did the thing everyone of his descendants would do for the next six thousand years.

He blamed somebody else.

"The woman whom thou gavest to be with me, she gave me of the tree, and I did eat."

Read that sentence slowly, because the move underneath it is the move that will follow you the rest of your life if you do not learn to spot it.

Adam blamed his wife. That was the obvious deflection. But look closer. Adam also blamed God. Listen to the pronoun—the *woman whom thou gavest to be with me.* The *thou* was aimed past Eve and laid at the feet of the One who had given Eve to him. He did not say, *I sinned, and I have no excuse.* He said, in effect, *If you had not given me this woman, I would not be standing here naked behind a tree.* The first sinful man on earth, in the first conversation he ever had after his sin, attempted to make God a quiet partner in his fall.

That was the very first time anyone ever did it. But it certainly was not the last.

Watch what happened next, because it shows you something important. Eve, when God turned and asked her, did exactly what her husband had just done. She blamed too. *"The serpent beguiled me, and I did eat"* (Genesis 3:13). Like Adam, she pointed at somebody else and tried to slide out from under the weight of it. Like Adam, she did not say, *I sinned, and I have no excuse.* She gestured at the snake the way Adam had gestured at her, and the way Adam had gestured at God.

It did not work for either of them.

God did not say, *Well, if Eve gave it to you, then you are off the hook.* God did not say, *Well, if the serpent tricked you, then I will let it slide.* He held every one of them accountable. He cursed the serpent. He brought sorrow to the woman. He drove them both from the garden. The blame-shifting did not lighten the consequences by even a single ounce. All it did was make sure that the first words out of the first sinners' mouths were understood to be lies.

If you want to know why James, two thousand years later, opens his teaching on temptation by ripping the favorite excuse out of your hand before you can use it, this is why. He had been watching it happen his whole life. He had seen his brothers do it. He had seen the early church do it. He knew that the moment you start talking honestly with people about their sin, the very first thing they will do is reach behind themselves for a tree to hide behind. The second thing they will do is blame somebody.

If they cannot blame anybody else, they will blame God.

So before James says one word about how temptation works, he speaks a word about where it does not come from.

"Let no man say when he is tempted, I am tempted of God: for God cannot be tempted with evil, neither tempteth he any man." (James 1:13)

There are three things to notice in this one verse, and we are going to look at them one at a time.

"Let No Man Say"

James knew you were going to say it because everyone seems to do it.

He didn't write *"don't think it"* or *"don't feel it."* He wrote, *"Don't say it."* He wrote it that way because he knew (by inspiration) that you were going to try. He knew the words were already forming in your mouth before you had even sinned, because they were forming in everybody's mouth.

You have said some version of these words. Maybe not out loud, but you have said them.

Why would God put a girl that pretty in my class if He didn't want me to look at her like that?

God knew my dad was going to be the way he is. He's the one who gave me this temper. What does He expect?

If God didn't want me to drink, He shouldn't have made it feel that good.

I prayed for help on Friday night, and He didn't help me, so what was I supposed to do?

God put that opportunity right in front of me. Why would He do that if He didn't mean for me to take it?

Every one of those sentences is a tree. Every one of them is a leaf stitched together. Every one of them is a man crouching behind something with his pulse hammering, trying to make himself small. Every one of them does the same thing Adam did. They take the responsibility, and they hand it back to God.

Sometimes the blame is loud, the way Adam's was, with God's name right there in the sentence. More often, the blame is quiet. It hides inside a complaint that sounds spiritual on the outside.

Why does this keep happening to me when I'm trying so hard?

If God really cared, He would have stopped me.

I asked Him to take this away years ago, and He still hasn't.

You can pray a sentence and accuse God in the same breath. You can grumble in His direction and call it a lament. You can tell yourself you are confused or hurting or just being honest about your struggle, when what is actually happening is that you are quietly making Him answer for what your own lust has done. That is the same move Adam made, just dressed up nicer.

James says no.

He says it before you have a chance to say anything else. He says it before he tells you a single thing about how temptation actually works. He says it first because the rest of what he is about to teach will not stick to a heart that still has even a little bit of God-blame within it. As long as you can pin even a sliver of the blame on God, you will always have an exit ramp out of your own repentance. James closes that ramp on the very first word.

"God Cannot Be Tempted with Evil"

James first makes this vital statement, then explains why.

Most of us have never thought about this part. We have never sat down and asked ourselves whether God Himself can be tempted. We assume God is too far above all of that to bother thinking about. James asks us to think about it for one verse, because the answer is so vital to us.

"God cannot be tempted with evil."

Stop on those words for a minute. They do not say *God refuses* or *God resists* or *God overcomes.* They say God *cannot.* The thing that pulls so hard on you has no pull on Him at all. The thing that you and I cannot stop circling holds zero fascination for the heart of God. There is nothing in evil that interests Him. No part of His nature leans toward it. There is no hidden corner of His being that has ever thought, *just for a second*, what it might be like to give in.

"God is light, and in him is no darkness at all" (1 John 1:5).

If God cannot be tempted with evil, then God will never use evil to tempt you. He cannot give you what He does not have. He cannot offer you what holds no value to Him. He cannot dangle a hook that He has no hand to dangle it with. The bait that pulled at you last night was not in His tackle box, because He does not own a tackle box like that.

When you blame God, then, you blame Him for something He physically cannot have done. You charge Him with a crime He is not capable of committing.

"Neither Tempteth He Any Man"

Now James says it plain.

God does not tempt. He never has, and He never will. Not yesterday. Not tomorrow. Not the night you fell. Not the morning you swore you would do better. God has never, in all of eternity, arranged a situation specifically to draw a human being toward sin.

This is the line you have to draw deep into the floor of your own heart, because the next chapters of this book will not work until this line holds.

But here is where some readers get confused, so let me handle a question before it grows into an objection.

The Bible does say that God tests people. He tested Abraham on the mountain with Isaac. He tested Israel in the wilderness with hunger and thirst. He tested Job by allowing the loss of everything that Job loved. James himself, eleven verses earlier, told you to count it all joy when you fall into all kinds of trials, because the trying of your faith works patience (James 1:2-3). So is God testing or not?

He is. But testing and tempting are not the same thing. Understanding the difference is vital for all of us.

A test from God is designed to make you stronger. A temptation from your own lust is designed to make you fall. The pressure may feel similar in the moment, but the difference lies in what's on the other side of it. A coach pushing you through one more set of sprints is not trying to wreck your knees; he is trying to build your legs and stamina. A friend pushing a beer into your hand at a party is not trying to build anything; he is trying to get you to drink. Same kind of pressure. Different source. Different goal.

When God tests you, the way out is to endure and grow. When your lust tempts you, the way out is to flee.

You can tell the difference because of where the pressure is pointing. A test points you toward God. A temptation points you away from Him. A test ends with you stronger. A temptation ends with you on the boards of the porch like the june bug.

Here is the promise that holds all of this together.

"There hath no temptation taken you but such as is common to man: but God is faithful, who will not suffer you to be tempted above that ye are able; but will with the temptation also make a way to escape, that ye may be able to bear it" (1 Corinthians 10:13).

God is not the source of the temptation. God is the One who provides the door out of it. He is the way of escape, not the trap.

Blame Him for the temptation, and you will not look for the door that He is holding open.

Application:

Let me try to make this easy to apply in your daily life.

The next time you sin, you will feel something move inside your chest that wants to deflect. You will feel words start to form that put the blame somewhere other than on you. They will sound reasonable. They will sound like a defense. They will sound like an explanation. Some of them might even contain a little truth, the way Adam's deflection contained a little truth. Eve really did hand him the fruit. God really did give him the woman. What he said was technically accurate, and it was still a lie, because what he said was an attempt to slide the responsibility off of his own shoulders and onto somebody else's.

The first move of repentance is to refuse to do that. The first move of repentance is to stop talking long enough to say the one true sentence about what just happened.

I sinned. I knew better. I did it anyway. It was me.

You will not believe how much power those four sentences have until you say them honestly. They cut every fig leaf you have stitched together. They remove every tree you have hidden behind. They strip the whole conversation down to what it always was: just you, just God, and just the truth.

The moment you stop blaming Him, you can finally start hearing what He has to say. **He has something to say.**

You will find, when you finally stop blaming Him, that He was never angry the way you thought He was. The God who walked through the garden looking for Adam was not stomping. He was searching. The voice that called *"Adam, where art thou?"* was the voice of a Father who had lost a son in the trees. He was not surprised. He was not unprepared. He was already moving toward the man with the rest of His plan in motion.

The same is true right now. The God you have been blaming is not crouched in some far corner of Heaven cataloging your failures and waiting to crush you. He is already walking toward you in the cool of the day. He is already calling your name. The only thing keeping you from hearing Him is the noise of your own deflection. Quiet that down, step out from behind the tree, and you will find Him much closer than you thought.

There is a reason this is chapter two in this book and not chapter twelve. There is a reason James puts this teaching first in his book. The rest of the road we are about to walk together depends on your willingness to take responsibility for what is happening inside of you every day. The pull. The bait. The conception. The birth. The death. Every stop on that road is going to ask you to own more, not less.

You cannot fight the pull if you think God is the one pulling.

You cannot dodge the bait if you think God is the one dangling it.

You cannot kill the lust inside of you if you think God is the one feeding it.

The whole road depends on the first stop being settled in your mind and heart. The first stop is settled when you stand up from behind the tree, walk out into the open air, look into the mirror of God's word, and stop blaming Him for what your own heart has done.

Adam never quite got there. He hid behind a tree, then he hid behind his wife, then he hid behind God, and God put him out of the garden anyway. But the same God who put him out of the garden made the first promise of the gospel inside that very same conversation, when He said the seed of the woman would one day crush the head of the serpent (Genesis 3:15). Even in the middle of the world's first blame-shift, God was already laying the groundwork to fix what Adam had broken.

That promise came true two thousand years ago on a hill outside Jerusalem. It is still true right now. Stop blaming Him, and you will find Him still standing right where He has always been, holding the door of escape open.

You can walk through it. Or you can keep crouching behind the tree.

The June bug on the porch never really had that choice. You do.

For Discussion:

1. Adam's deflection in Genesis 3:12 was technically accurate. Eve really did give him the fruit, and God really did give him Eve. So why does the author call it a lie? What was Adam actually doing with that sentence?

2. James 1:13 starts with the words *"Let no man say."* Why do you think James addresses what we *say* about temptation before he addresses anything else? What does this tell you about how often this excuse comes up?

3. Read the loud examples and the quiet examples in the section under *"Let No Man Say."* Which kind do you find yourself reaching for more often, the loud blame or the quiet, prayer-shaped kind? Why is the quiet kind harder to spot?

4. Explain in your own words the difference between a *test* from God and a *temptation* from your own lust. Why does it matter that you can tell them apart?

5. The author writes that the first move of repentance is the sentence *"I sinned. I knew better. I did it anyway. It was me."* When was the last time you said something like that out loud? What gets in the way of saying it?

6. 1 Corinthians 10:13 promises that God always provides a *"way to escape"* from temptation. If God is the One holding the door open, what does it cost you when you accuse Him of being the one who shut you in the room?

Chapter 3

Drawn Away

The pond was as still as glass at sunrise, the kind of stillness we can only get in the first thirty minutes after dawn before the wind picks up. The water was the color of weak coffee, dark from the runoff of a recent rain and the leaves on the bottom, and you could not see two feet down into it. A beautiful heron stood ankle-deep on the far bank, motionless, doing what herons do. Out in the middle, a turtle's nose broke the surface for a second, then was gone.

I stood on the bank with a fishing rod in my hand and a topwater lure tied to ten-pound braided line. The lure was a buzzbait about the size of my thumb, painted to look like a wounded bream, with a little metal propeller on the back that would sputter and click when I reeled it across the surface. I knew where the fish was. I had caught him out from under the same log three different times last summer. I knew the cast it would take, and I knew the retrieve to reel. I had been thinking about him for a week.

The bass was under that log at that very moment. He was a largemouth bass, about five pounds, dark green on the back, fading to white on the belly. He was holding in the shade where the log met the water, just barely finning to keep himself in place. He had been in that exact spot since before the sun came up. From down there in the dark, the world above the water was a soft, blurred ceiling of light. He could see motion overhead and feel vibration through the water. Other than that, his world was small and dark and safe.

I flipped the lure ten feet past the log and started reeling. The buzzbait hit the surface and started doing what it was built to do, sputtering across the calm water, throwing a small wake behind it, pretending to be something hurt and easy to catch.

The bass felt it before he saw it. The vibration changed something in him, and he turned his head a quarter inch toward the surface. He should not have. He was fine where he was. He had everything he needed under that log. But something in him moved.

The buzzbait sputtered closer. The bass eased forward an inch. He had not committed yet. He could still go back. But his nose was now out of the deepest shadow, and his pectoral fins were doing more than just holding him in place. They were nudging him. They were moving him.

Two feet from the log, the bass made his decision. He shot up. The water exploded. The buzzbait disappeared in a foam of white and green, and I set the hook hard.

The fish did everything a five-pound bass does when it realizes it has made a mistake. He shook his head. He ran for the log. He jumped, twisting in the air with the lure flashing in his open mouth. He tried to throw the hook, and he tried to break the line, and he tried to bury himself in the brush at the bottom of the pond. None of it worked. I walked him slowly in. I eased him up onto the bank. I held him in my wet hand and looked at the lure planted firmly in the corner of his mouth and listened to him gasp and felt the weight of him.

He had been safe under the log five minutes earlier. Now he was on the bank.

That is *exelkomenos*.

The Meaning of *"Drawn Away"*

The Greek word James uses for *"drawn away"* in James 1:14 is *exelkomenos*. It comes from a verb that means to drag out, to haul out, to pull out from a hiding place. It is the kind of word a fisherman or a hunter uses. You draw a bass out from the cover of the log. You lure a deer out of the brush. You pull something out of where it was supposed to be and into the open, where it is exposed.

Open the verse again, with that bass in mind.

> *"But every man is tempted, when he is drawn away of his own lust, and enticed."* (James 1:14)

The bass was under cover. He was supposed to stay there. Something on the surface caught his attention, and he turned his head. He eased forward. He committed. I set the hook.

Notice that James does not say the Devil draws the man away. He says the man is drawn away of his *own lust*. The thing that pulled the bass out from under the log was not the lure. The lure could sputter all morning over an empty pond, and nothing would happen. The thing that pulled the bass out was something inside the bass that responded to the lure. The hunger. The instinct to chase. The little switch in his head that said *go*. The lure was real, but the lure could not have done a thing without the bass's own pull on the inside.

That is the distinction we drew in the last chapter, and it is the one we have to keep drawing for the rest of this book. Bait without lust does nothing. Lust without bait still sits inside you, waiting. The two of them have to meet to begin the pull.

When the meeting happens, you get drawn away.

The very first sin in human history started this way. The serpent did his talking, and then Eve looked.

> *"And when the woman saw that the tree was good for food, and that it was pleasant to the eyes, and a tree to be desired to make one wise, she took of the fruit thereof, and did eat..."* (Genesis 3:6)

She saw the fruit. Then she desired it. Then she took it.

Read it slowly. Eve did not jump from standing around the tree doing nothing to eating the fruit in a single motion. Something in between happened. She turned her head. She looked. She looked again. She let her eyes rest on the fruit long enough to start cataloging what was good about it. *Good for food. Pleasant to the eyes. To be desired to make one wise.* That is the sound of a woman being drawn away. She had not eaten yet. She had not even reached out her hand. But her insides had already started moving toward the tree.

The taking came after the looking. The looking came after the turning of the head. The turning of the head came after the serpent's question. The whole thing was already in motion long before the fruit ever touched her lips.

The same is true of every sin you have ever committed. The eating is fifth in line. The looking is somewhere around second.

Solomon understood this so well that he wrote an entire chapter of Proverbs about it. He sat at his window one evening and watched a young man walk into a trap. He wrote down what he saw, and the description still cuts.

> *"For at the window of my house I looked through my casement, and beheld among the simple ones, I discerned among the youths, a young man void of understanding, passing through the street near her corner; and he went the way to her house..."* (Proverbs 7:6-8)

The young man did not have to walk down that particular street. He could have taken any number of other routes home. But he walked the one that took him past her corner. That was the first turn of his head. He had not done anything yet. He had just started drifting, the way the bass drifted, in the direction of the bait.

Then she came out. She talked sweetly to him. She told him her husband was out of town and would not be back for a long time, and that the bed was already prepared. Solomon writes down the whole conversation, and then he writes one of the most haunting sentences in the Old Testament about what happened to that young man.

"He goeth after her straightway, as an ox goeth to the slaughter, or as a fool to the correction of the stocks; till a dart strike through his liver; as a bird hasteth to the snare, and knoweth not that it is for his life." (Proverbs 7:22-23)

Solomon gives us three pictures in two verses. The ox going to the slaughterhouse. The bird flying into the trap. The fool walking into the stocks. None of them knows what is about to happen. None of them feels the fall coming. They are just walking. They are just turning their heads. They are just doing what a young man does when something on the corner has caught his eye.

That is exactly how it works. That is what drawn away looks like with skin on.

Application:

I will try to make this easy to apply in your daily life here.

You are not going to feel a great clanging alarm bell in your chest when the pull starts. You are not going to hear a voice in your head warning you that this is the moment. The pull does not announce itself. It is much smaller than that. It is the size of a quarter-inch turn of the head.

Here is what the pull actually looks like, in your week, this week.

The notification lights up your screen at eleven thirty at night, and you tell yourself you will just check it.

The conversation in the hallway turns slightly off-color, and you do not walk away.

The girl who is not your girlfriend smiles at you on Sunday, and you start noticing where she is sitting on Wednesday.

The video pops up in your feed that you wouldn't show your dad, and you tell yourself you are just curious about what it is.

The friend who you know gets you in trouble texts you on Friday afternoon, and you do not write back yet, but you sit there looking at the screen.

The thought arrives in your head while you are trying to fall asleep, and you do not throw it out. You let it sit there. You turn it over. You look at the shape of it.

Every one of those is a quarter-inch turn of the head. Every one of those is the bass beginning to move out from under the log. None of them is a sin yet. None of them is even close to sin yet, in the sense of an act you have committed. But every one of them is the first stop on a road that James has already described, and that ends, every time, with a body on the boards, just like the june bug or the big bass under the log.

The terrible thing about this stop is that most Christians do not know they are on it. They think the road starts at stop five, where the act happens. They think the only part of all of this worth fighting is the act. So they walk through stops one, two, three, and four with their guard down, telling themselves they are not really sinning, telling themselves they are still in control. By the time the act arrives, they have been baited and dragged out of cover for so long that they are no longer really making a decision. They are just doing what the previous four stops have already prepared them to do.

The fight is here. The fight is at the quarter-inch turn.

So why don't we recognize it when it happens?

There are three reasons.

The first is that the pull does not feel like sin. It feels like curiosity. It feels like interest. It feels like a passing thought. *I'm not doing anything. I'm just looking. I'm just thinking about it. I'm not committing to anything.* Every one of those sentences is true in the smallest possible sense. None of them is true in the sense that matters. The pull is not yet sin, but the pull is the seam where sin gets in. Letting the pull run is how you end up on the bank.

The second is that we have been taught wrong. We have been taught that the only thing that counts is the act. Stay a virgin until you get married. Don't get drunk. Don't steal. Don't curse. So our whole framework for fighting sin is built around the moment of action. We do not have a category for the pull because nobody ever taught us to fight at the pull. James is teaching us a category right now. The category is *drawn away.* If you can name it, you can fight it.

The third takeaway is that admitting the pull is real means admitting we have a problem. As long as you can tell yourself you are not really being tempted, only looking, only thinking, only curious, you do not have to deal with the lust underneath. The minute you admit that the pull on you is a real pull, you have to ask the harder question of what is alive in you that responds to it. That is the question we will spend the next chapter on. Most of us would rather not ask it.

So we leave the pull unnamed, and the bass keeps drifting toward the lure, and the pattern keeps repeating.

Here is the thing nobody tells you about the pull.

The first moment of it is when you have the most leverage over the situation. Every second after that is a second harder.

The bass that turned his head a quarter inch could have turned it back. It would have taken almost nothing. A heartbeat of focus, and he could have settled back into the shade, and the buzzbait could have sputtered on by, and that would have been the end of it. But every moment and every inch that he eased forward made the next inch that much easier. By the time he was two feet away from the log, the part of him that wanted to chase the lure had drowned out the part of him that wanted to stay safe. The decision was already made.

You are the same way.

The notification you do not pick up at eleven thirty is the easiest one to not pick up. Once you have unlocked the screen, a smaller part of you is in charge of what happens next. The conversation you walk away from in the first five seconds is the easiest one to walk away from. Once you have laughed at the first joke, you have signaled that you are staying, and the next joke is easier to laugh at. The thought you throw out in the first second is the easiest one to throw out. Once you have let it sit in your head for a full minute, you have given it a chair to sit in.

Watch the first second. Watch the first turn of the head. That is where the leverage is. That is where the whole battle, in a real sense, gets won or lost.

You will not always get this right. Nobody does. But you will start getting it right more often the day you start noticing it at all. The bass that learns to feel the lure coming from far away is the bass that lives long enough to be old.

Here is what the next few chapters are going to do.

We are going to look at the lust that responds to the bait. We are going to look at the bait itself. We are going to look at what happens inside the heart at the moment of agreement, at the act, and at the death the act gives birth to. This chapter has just opened the road. The pull is the first stop, and we will spend the rest of the book learning the road from that first stop onwards.

But before you turn the page, sit with this thought for a minute.

Think back through your last week. Think about the moments your head turned like the bass to the buzzbait. Think about the conversations you did not walk away from, the videos you did not close, the screens you did not put down, the thoughts you did not throw out. None of those was the act. None of those were what your conscience would mark down as sin. But every one of them was a fish easing out from under a log toward something that was sputtering across the surface above him.

Some of those stories ended with you on the bank. Some of them ended with you back under the log just in time. Either way, you can see the pull now if you look for it. That is the beginning of fighting back.

The June bug on the porch never had the chance to learn this. He was wired all the way through, and he never knew he was being drawn. You are different. You have been given a Bible that names what is happening to you, and you have been given the room to fight at the first quarter-inch.

Use it.

Discussion Questions:

1. Read Genesis 3:6 again. What is the order of what happens to Eve before she eats the fruit? Where does *" Drawn Away " show* up in that sequence?

2. In Proverbs 7, the young man *"passes through the street near her corner."* Why does the author point out that the road home was not the only road he could have taken? When is the last time you took a road you knew you should not be on?

3. Name three "quarter-inch turns of the head" you noticed in yourself this week. What were they? Why did you turn?

4. The chapter says the first second of the pull is when you have the most leverage. Why do you think that is true? What happens to your ability to fight the pull as the seconds go by?

5. The author lists three reasons we don't recognize the pull when it happens: (1) it doesn't feel like sin, (2) we've been taught only the act counts, and (3) admitting the pull means admitting a deeper problem. Which one do you think gets you most often?

6. James says you *are drawn away of your own lust*. What does that mean for how seriously you should take the pull when you feel it? Whose responsibility is it to fight at the first second?

Chapter 4

Your Own Lust

The Israelites had just walked across the dry bed of the Jordan River. They had watched the walls of Jericho fall flat at the sound of seven priests blowing seven trumpets. God had told one thing very plainly before the city ever came down. The silver, the gold, the brass, and the iron belonged only to God, and the whole city was under the ban. Touch nothing. Take nothing. The firstfruits of Canaan belonged to the Lord, and Israel was not to lay a finger on them.

A man named Achan walked through the smoke after the trumpets stopped. He stepped over the rubble of a city wall that had stood for centuries that morning, and by lunch, it was a pile of broken stones. He passed bodies. He passed broken pottery. He passed houses that had been split open like dropped melons. Somewhere in the wreckage of a wealthy man's house, he saw three things that froze him in his tracks.

He saw a Babylonian garment, embroidered with thread he could not have afforded in three years of work. He saw two hundred shekels of silver. He saw a wedge of gold weighing about a pound and a quarter.

He looked at them for a long time.

Then he wrapped them up. He carried them back to his tent. He dug a hole under the floor of where his family slept. He buried them. He told himself it was nothing. The Lord had given Israel the whole city. What did a little bit of cloth and metal matter compared to that?

Then Israel marched up to the next town. It was a small place called Ai. It should have fallen in less than an afternoon. Instead, the Israelites were chased back by the men of Ai, and thirty-six of them died on the way down the hill. Joshua tore his clothes, fell on his face before the Lord, and asked what had happened. The Lord told him plainly that there was sin in the camp.

Joshua brought the tribes through the tribes, then the families, then the households, then the individual men. Achan was caught. Standing in front of the whole nation, with his sin exposed in front of God and everybody, Achan made one of the cleanest, most clinical confessions in the entire Old Testament.

> *"When I saw among the spoils a goodly Babylonish garment, and two hundred shekels of silver, and a wedge of gold of fifty shekels weight, then I coveted them, and took them; and, behold, they are hid in the earth in the midst of my tent..."* (Joshua 7:21)

I Saw...I Coveted...I Took...

Three verbs in fourteen words. *I saw. I coveted. I took.*

Read it again, slowly. Achan, standing there with the men of Israel about to put him to death, did not say *the Devil made me do it*. He did not say *the city of Jericho was just too rich for any man to walk through*. He did not say *I never had a chance*. He gave the clearest description of the anatomy of sin in the entire book of Joshua and, arguably, the entire Bible. He saw. He coveted. He took.

The middle verb is the one that breaks the door open. *I coveted.* That was not a problem produced in the city of Jericho. That was a problem that was already in him. The garment did not leap from the rubble pile and force itself into Achan's hands. The garment was just lying there. The silver was just lying there. The gold was just lying there. None of it could have done a thing without an Achan walking by who had the kind of heart that wanted those things more than he wanted to obey.

The bait was in Jericho. But the lust was in him.

The Lust Problem

That is what James describes in the second half of verse fourteen. He has already told you the pull is real. He has already told you the bait is real. Now he tells you where the problem of the whole thing actually lives.

> *"But every man is tempted, when he is drawn away of his own lust, and enticed."* (James 1:14)

Of his own lust. Not the world's lust pressed onto him from outside. Not the Devil's lust transferred into him by magic. Not God's bad design that gave him a sinful nature and then blamed him for using it. *His own.*

The Greek word here is *epithumia*. It means a strong desire, a craving, a pull toward something. It does not always have to be sinful in itself. The same Greek root shows up when Jesus says, *"With desire I have desired to eat this Passover with you before I suffer"* (Luke 22:15). Strong desire can be holy when it is directed at the right object. The problem is that, in people, the desire keeps pointing to things God has placed off-limits. It keeps reaching past the boundary line. It keeps wanting what does not belong to it.

Every man deals with it. Every woman with it. Every preacher's kid and every elder's wife and every quiet, sweet little old lady who seems like a perfect saint in the third pew on the left has to deal with it. The lust we struggle with is part of what came with the sin problem in us all when Adam and Eve walked out of the garden, and it has been at work in every human heart born since.

The question is not whether you will have to deal with lust. The question is what shape your lust will take and where you will allow it to take you.

Internal Filth

Jesus said it very plainly one afternoon to a crowd of his disciples and a group of Pharisees who were arguing with him about clean and unclean food. He said the food they ate was not what was making them filthy. The filth was already inside them, and it just kept coming out.

> *"For from within, out of the heart of men, proceed evil thoughts, adulteries, fornications, murders, thefts, covetousness, wickedness, deceit, lasciviousness, an evil eye, blasphemy, pride, foolishness: All these evil things come from within, and defile the man."* (Mark 7:21-23)

Read that list slowly. Every one of those things has a starting place. The starting place is not the world out there. The starting place is *the heart.* Adultery starts there. Covetousness starts there. Pride starts there. Lasciviousness starts there. Murder starts there. The whole catalog of human evil has one address, and the address is on the inside of you.

That should change the way you fight against temptation.

If your sin really did come from outside, then all you would ever need to do is run far enough away from the bait to be safe. You could move to a different state. You could change schools. You could throw your phone in the river and live in a cabin in the woods. And if you ever found a place quiet enough and clean enough, the lust would go away because it had nothing left to feed on.

But that is not how all of this works. You can take a sinner to a desert, and he will lust after sand. Lock him in a monastery, and he will find something to lust after. Send him to the moon, and he will figure out a way to lust there, too. The bait might change. The shapes might shift. The lust travels with him because the lust is in him.

Jeremiah said it five hundred years before Jesus did:

"The heart is deceitful above all things, and desperately wicked: who can know it?" (Jeremiah 17:9)

The heart of a man cannot be trusted. The heart of a Christian, even with the new life of Christ in him, will still throw up reminders of the old man until the day he dies. Paul wrote a whole chapter about that fight in Romans 7. He found himself doing what he did not want to do, and he traced the problem all the way back inside himself, where the law of sin was still working in his members. The struggle did not end the day he was baptized. It changed shape and gained new power through Christ, but it did not vanish.

Yours has not vanished either. That is why you are reading this book.

Here is where Christians get into trouble. They are willing to admit that the bait is real and that the pull is real. What they do not want to admit is that the lust is real, and that it lives in them, and that it has its own shape and its own appetites that did not come from anywhere out there. Don't make this mistake, though – God did not put your lust inside you. It developed over the course of your life from what you allowed inside of you.

So you will hear something like this:

"I would never have been tempted if she had not worn that dress."

"I never used to have a problem with this until I started working at that office."

"I was fine until my friends got me into it."

Listen to the movement here. Every one of those sentences pretends that the lust would not exist if the bait had not shown up. Every one of them puts the engine on the outside, where the speaker does not have to do the harder work. Every one of them is technically partly true, in the same way Adam was technically partly true. The dress was real. The office was real. The friends were real. None of those statements is a lie about the world. They are all lies about the heart.

The lust was already in you. The bait just gave it something to land on.

You can prove it to yourself with one question: if you took the bait away, would the lust go away? Take the dress away, change the office, change the friends, and watch what happens. Watch where your eyes go next. Watch what your imagination does in the quiet hours. Watch what your mind reaches for when nothing in particular is on the screen. The lust will not have evaporated. It will have looked for a new place to land because it lives in you.

Application:

You have a particular shape of lust. So do I. So does the boy in the pew next to you, the girl on your bus to school, and the man you respect most in your congregation. Every Christian carries a particular cluster of cravings that have been at work in their heart, and the cluster is not the same as anybody else's. Some Christians struggle most with sexual lust. Some struggle most with anger. Some struggle most with pride, or money, or food, or the desperate need to be liked. Some struggle most with the slow, quiet sin of resentment toward people in their own family.

You know what your shape is, even if you have never said it out loud. You know what reaches you fastest when you are tired, hungry, or alone. You know which baits land on you and which ones float by without ever catching your eye. You have known your shape for a long time.

Most Christians are afraid to name it.

Naming it feels like admitting it has more power over them than they want to admit. So they leave it unnamed. They leave it in the dark. They use vague words like *struggling* or *issues* or *not where I want to be*, and they never quite say the specific thing out loud. The lust loves that. The lust thrives in the dark. The lust grows like mold on the underside of words that never get spoken.

The first thing you have to do, after you have stopped blaming God (chapter two) and after you have noticed the pull (chapter three), is name what is in you that responds to the bait when it lands nearby.

Not in general vague terms. This work needs to be specific.

Not - *I have some struggles*. Instead - *I lust after women I see in the produce aisle of the grocery store.*

Not - *I get a little angry sometimes*. Instead - *I have an absolute fury toward my father that I have never gotten rid of, and it leaks out every time he calls.*

Not - *I'm not where I want to be on the phone.* Instead - *I cannot stop scrolling for 30 minutes once I have started, and the things I scroll past are not things I would let my mother read.*

Read those three pairs again. The vague version protects the lust. The specific version exposes it. You cannot fight what you will not name. You cannot kill what you will not look at. You cannot bring to God what you will not put into words.

There is a reason 1 John 1:9 says, *"If we confess our sins, he is faithful and just to forgive us our sins, and to cleanse us from all unrighteousness."* The verb is *confess. Homologeō* in Greek. It means the same thing as *'to agree with'.* To put your words next to God's words about the same thing. Confession is not a vague apology. Confession is naming the lust the way God names it, in the words God uses, with the specificity God uses.

When was the last time you did that?

Achan's confession was clean because it was specific. He named the garment. He named the silver. He named the gold. He named the weights. He named the place where he had buried it. He told the people gathered that day exactly what was in his heart and exactly what his heart had done with what it saw. There was no fog in his confession. There was no wiggle room. There were three verbs and a body of evidence.

His confession did not save his life, though. The judgment of the Lord on him was final, and the men of Israel stoned him and his household in the valley of Achor that same day. But his confession is in the Bible four thousand years later, and one of the reasons it is in there is so the rest of us can learn from it. The cleanness of it. The honesty of it. The way he laid the lust down in front of the crowd without a single excuse.

You can confess like that. You can name the lust in you that has been hiding under the floor of your tent for years. You can speak it out loud to God, and to the people who love you in Christ enough to hear it, and you can stop pretending it is not there.

When you do that, the lust loses power over you. Not all of its power, not yet. But it loses the power that came from being unnamed. It loses the power of the darkness. It comes up out of the floor of your tent into the light of day, and you can finally see what you have been carrying around all this time.

Here is where the next chapter is going. We have looked at the source of the pull, which is your own lust. We are about to look at the bait that meets the lust, which James calls being *enticed*. We will see what makes a particular bait work on a particular lust, and we will see why the same hook that catches one bass leaves another one alone. The lust and the bait are two different things, and you have to learn to see them as two different things if you are going to fight them as two different things.

But before you turn the page, sit with what is inside of you for a minute.

Stop telling yourself that your sin is mostly out there. Stop blaming the dress, the office, the friends, and the phone. Stop blaming your parents and your past and your circumstances and the country you grew up in. Some of those things are real. But not a one of them is the engine. The engine has been in your chest your whole life, and right now is a good time to start saying that out loud.

You will be amazed at how much lighter you will feel when you stop carrying the lie that all of this is somebody else's fault.

The June bug never had to do this work. The June bug never had a heart that could be honest about itself. He flew at the light because that was all he was. The same is true for the bass under the log. They are just soulless insects and animals that are driven by instinct. You are not all you are. You are a soul made in the image of God, ruined by the fall, called by the gospel, and being remade in the image of His Son. That last part is real. But it cannot do its work in you while you are still pretending the lust is not there.

Name it. Bring it up out of the floor of the tent. Lay it in front of the Lord.

That is the third stop on the road, and that is where the rest of this book begins.

Discussion Questions:

1. Read Joshua 7:20-21. Why does the author say Achan's confession is one of the cleanest in the Bible? What does the specificity of his confession teach you about your own?

2. Jesus says in Mark 7:21-23 that evil comes *out of* the heart, not *into* the heart. How does this change the way you have to fight your sin? Why is fighting only the bait not enough?

3. The chapter says every Christian has a particular shape of lust. Without writing it down where anyone else can see, can you name yours specifically and out loud? What gets in the way of doing so?

4. Look at the three vague-versus-specific pairs in the application section. Have you ever caught yourself using the vague version? Why is the vague version actually more dangerous than the specific one?

5. Read 1 John 1:9 and look up the Greek word *homologeō*. What does it mean to *say the same thing as God* about your sin? When was the last time you did that?

6. Take the bait away in your imagination. If your phone, your job, and your circle of friends were all changed tomorrow, what would your lust still want? What does that tell you about where the engine actually lives?

Chapter 5

Enticed

Jesus had not eaten in forty days.

He had walked out into the wilderness somewhere east of the Jordan after his baptism, and he had been there alone for almost six weeks. The terrain was hard. It was the kind of country that gave a man little. Bare rock. Thorn bushes. A sun that does not let up. At night, the temperature could drop into the forties. During the day, it could climb past a hundred. There were jackals out there, and snakes, and the kinds of animals Mark mentions almost in passing when he says Jesus *"was with the wild beasts"* (Mark 1:13).

The text says he ate nothing during those forty days, and at the end of them, he was hungry.

That is one of the great understatements of the Bible. A man who has gone forty days without food is not *hungry* the way you and I are hungry at five o'clock waiting for supper to be put on the table. A man who has gone forty days without food is in the late stages of starvation. His body has eaten through its fat reserves. It has started devouring its own muscles. His mind is foggy. His joints ache. The smell of bread, even the suggestion of bread, surely would have been almost unbearable.

That is when the tempter showed up.

He was not subtle. He did not waste any time. He looked at the man whose bones were starting to show through his skin, and he made his first offer.

> *"And when the tempter came to him, he said, If thou be the Son of God, command that these stones be made bread."* (Matthew 4:3)

Look at that bait carefully. It is not a generic temptation. It is not a lazy stone thrown in the general direction of the Lord. It is custom-tied to the situation and to the man. The tempter knew Jesus was hungry. He could see the rocks at his feet. They were the small, round, loaf-shaped stones that lay all over that wilderness, the size of a small loaf of bread, the color of a small loaf of bread. They sat right in front of Jesus like a baker's display. *Just turn these into what they already look like, and eat. You have the power. You have the right. Why are you starving when you are the Son of God?*

That is the bait. That is the Greek word *deleazomenos.*

Jesus said no, and then he answered with one verse from Deuteronomy.

> *"Man shall not live by bread alone, but by every word that proceedeth out of the mouth of God"* (Matthew 4:4).

The bait did not hook Jesus.

So, the tempter tried again. He took Jesus to the pinnacle of the temple in Jerusalem, set him on the high corner where a man could see straight down 150 feet to the stones below, and quoted Psalm 91 back to him. *Throw yourself down. The Father will catch you. The angels will bear you up. Prove who you are.*

Jesus said no again.

The tempter tried a third time. He showed him all the kingdoms of the world in a moment, and he offered every one of them to Jesus on one condition. *Bow down to me, and all of this is yours. You will not have to go to the cross to get it. You will not have to die. Just kneel.*

Jesus said no a third time, and the tempter left him.

That is one of the most important scenes in the New Testament for what we are about to talk about. Three baits. Three custom-tied lures. Three appeals to what would have looked like real desires for a real man on a real mission. Every one of them missed, because in the soul of Jesus there was no lust to meet them.

The bait was real. The lust was not. And so the hook found nothing to grab.

This is what James means when he writes...

"But every man is tempted, when he is drawn away of his own lust, and enticed." (James 1:14)

The Greek word for *enticed* is *deleazomenos.* It is the second of two fishing words James uses in this verse, paired with *exelkomenos* in the line before it. *Exelkomenos* is the dragging out. *Deleazomenos* is the baiting. It comes from the noun *delear*, which means 'bait'. The worm on the hook. The fly on the leader. The deer corn in the feeder. The thing you put in front of an animal to get it close enough for the trap to work.

The bait, by definition, is designed to *look* like something good.

A worm on a hook does not look like a hook. It looks like a worm, which is what the bass eats every day. A fly tied at the vise does not just look like a fly tied at the vise. It looks like a real mayfly hatching off the surface of the river, which is what the trout has been feeding on all morning. The deer corn in the feeder does not look like a tool of a hunter. It looks like food, set out by no one in particular, free for the taking.

The whole point of bait is that the trap is hidden or at least unnoticed. The whole genius of bait is that the dangerous thing is dressed up in clothes that look exactly like the safe thing.

That is why bait works. It is not because the animal is stupid. It is because the bait is dressed to look appetizing.

Baited Temptation

Eve's first temptation was a baited temptation. The serpent did not walk up to her with a sign that said, *I am here to ruin your life and end the world as you know it.* He came as a creature that the text says was *more subtil than any beast of the field which the Lord God had made* (Genesis 3:1). He started with a question. *Yea, hath God said, Ye shall not eat of every tree of the garden?* (Genesis 3:1). The question was the bait. The question made Eve start thinking about the rules, whether they were fair, and whether God had really said what she thought He had.

Then he made his pitch.

> *"Ye shall not surely die: For God doth know that in the day ye eat thereof, then your eyes shall be opened, and ye shall be as gods, knowing good and evil."* (Genesis 3:4-5)

Look at the dress on that bait. The serpent did not say, *come, eat the fruit and ruin yourselves and your children and the whole world for thousands of years.* He said, *"Eat this and become more.* He took the most poisonous fruit on the planet and dressed it up in a garment of self-improvement. He took the path of cosmic ruin and dressed it up as the path of enlightenment. He took *no* and dressed it up as *more.*

That is what bait does. That is what bait has always done. This deception is the whole game.

The first time you sinned the way you sin now, the dress on the bait was probably this. *Just this once. Nobody will know. It will not hurt anything. You can stop whenever you want. Everybody else does it.* Read those five sentences. There are five different cuts of the same suit, and the suit is the safe thing. The dangerous thing is hiding inside. The dress is what made the dangerous thing look reachable.

If the dress had ever come off, you would not have touched the bait. If the screen had said, *Click here to start a habit that will last fifteen years and damage your future marriage*, you would not have clicked. If the cup had said, *drink me to start a relationship with alcohol that will end with your children losing respect for you*, you would not have drunk that first drink. If the late-night message had said, *answer me to lose your purity in three weeks and your reputation in six*, you would not have answered.

The bait does not dress like that, though. The bait dresses like the thing you wanted all along.

Dressed Up Bait

Let me show you some of the dresses your bait wears.

The dress of *just one more time*. This one is the most common. It tells you that one more click, one more drink, one more lap around the bug zapper is not really that big of a deal, and that this time will be the last. It is a lie every time. There has not been a *just one more time* in the history of human sin that has actually been the last one. I have fished for years. I play this game with myself. I am about ready to quit fishing for the day, and I will say *Just one more cast.* But it's never just one more cast, and I know it. *Just one more time*, is the dress that the next ten years are wearing.

There is also the dress of *I deserve this.* This one shows up after a hard day, after a hard week, or after a hard season of life. It tells you that you have earned a little break from the rules. You worked hard. You held the line a long time. Now you can let yourself have the thing you have been holding back from. This dress is reasonable on the outside. The dress is rebellious on the inside. The Lord did not give you the rules so you could break them when you felt tired.

The dress of *nobody will get hurt*. This one is the favorite of secret sins. It tells you that what happens in your own head, on your own screen, in your own private moments, does not affect anybody else. It is a flat lie. There is no such thing as a private sin. Every sin you have ever committed in private has changed the man or woman you are in public, and the people in your life have been receiving the leftovers of that change without knowing where it came from.

The dress of *this is just who I am*. This one is the lie of identity. It tells you that lust is part of your makeup, that it cannot be fought, that you have to integrate it instead of crucifying it. It uses the language of your culture to drape an old sin in new clothes. The Bible is not impressed by the new clothes. The Bible says crucify it. The Bible says put it to death. The Bible has never once told a Christian to make peace with what is killing him spiritually.

The dress of *God will forgive me*. This one is the most spiritual-looking and the most damaging. It uses grace as a license. It looks at the cross of Christ and decides that the cross has made sin cheap. Paul saw this dress coming a long way off. He wrote a whole chapter against it. *"Shall we continue in sin, that grace may abound? God forbid"* (Romans 6:1-2). The grace of God is not a coupon for the next sin. It is the power that breaks the lust at the root.

Each one of those is a dress. Each one of those covers a hook. The hook is going to do its work the moment your mouth closes on what looks like the worm.

Here is what makes this chapter different from the last one.

In the last chapter, we said the lust is yours. That is still true. The lust is the engine. Without the lust, the bait does nothing.

But the bait is not nothing either.

If the lust is the engine, the bait is the steering wheel. The lust by itself produces a generalized hunger inside you. The bait gives the hunger a shape. The bait gives lust an address. The bait says, *you can satisfy what is in you by reaching for what is in front of you.* And it lies. Every single time it lies. Because what is in front of you is never going to satisfy what is in you. It is going to feed it for a few minutes and leave it hungrier than before.

Solomon said it five hundred years before Christ:

> *"Hell and destruction are never full; so the eyes of man are never satisfied."* (Proverbs 27:20)

Whatever the bait promises you tonight, it cannot deliver tomorrow. The lust will be back. The bait will need a stronger version next time. The dress will get more elaborate. The hook will get bigger. That is how the road runs. Every drink calls for a stronger drink. Every video calls for a more shocking video. Every angry word at home calls for a louder one. The bait has to escalate because the lust never stays satisfied.

This is why the men and women who think they can manage their sin and not kill it always lose. Sin will not stay where you put it. Sin will not be domesticated. Sin will not be content with the corner of your life that you wanted to keep for it. It will spread. It will require more. It will turn from a private indulgence into a public ruin, given enough time. The bait will keep upgrading until you have nothing left it can upgrade to.

Application:

Today, when the bait shows up, do this one thing first. Before you do anything else, ask one question. *What is this bait dressed as?*

The notification is dressed as a connection. What is it really?

The video is dressed as entertainment. What is it really?

The message from the friend is dressed as fun. What is it really?

The drink at the party is dressed as freedom. What is it really?

The thought in your head at midnight is dressed as harmless. What is it really?

Please do not ask the question to find a clever answer. You are asking the question to strip the bait of its dress. If you can see the bait without its deceptive cloak, even for a few seconds, the pull on you will weaken dramatically. Because what looked like the thing you wanted will start looking like exactly what it is, which is a hook with a worm wrapped around it.

The serpent's lie about the fruit was that eating it would make Eve like God. The truth was that eating it would make her like a corpse. *In the day that thou eatest thereof thou shalt surely die* (Genesis 2:17). Once you have stripped the dress off the lie, the choice between *being like God* and *dying* is not really a choice anymore. The fruit only looks good while the dress is on.

Jesus did this in the wilderness. Watch how. Every time the tempter came at him with a piece of bait, Jesus did not negotiate with the bait. He did not look at the stones and consider whether one little loaf would really be that bad. He did not stand on the temple and weigh whether a small jump might be permissible. He answered the bait with the Word of God every single time, because the Word of God exposes the bait for what it is faster than anything else in the universe.

The Word said *man shall not live by bread alone.* That exposed the first lure. Hunger does not give you the right to disobey God.

The Word said *thou shalt not tempt the Lord thy God.* That exposed the second lure. Showing off your faith to prove who you are is not faith.

The Word said *thou shalt worship the Lord thy God, and him only shalt thou serve.* That exposed the truth of the third lure. Power gained by bowing to anyone other than God is not power.

Three baits. Three Words. Three exposures. Three escapes.

You have the same Word in your hands. The same Word that did the work in the wilderness will do the work in your bedroom and your office and your truck cab and your lonely Friday night. But you have to know it well enough to use it when the bait shows up. We will spend a chapter on that toward the end of the book.

The next chapter takes us to the dangerous space that opens up after the pull and the bait have met. James does not name this space directly, but it is in the picture he paints. It is the space between *drawn away and enticed*, and when *lust hath conceived.* It is the slow circle of the bug zapper. It is the lap before the final lap. It is what the June bug does for those last few minutes before the contact. Most Christians lose right here, and most Christians do not even know there is a *here* to lose at.

Before you turn the page, look at the dresses.

The bait that has been working on you for years has been wearing a dress for years. You have agreed to the dress for years. You have looked past the dress and pretended what was inside it was something good for so long that you have almost forgotten there was anything bad inside it at all. This is a good moment to look at the dress, name what it is hiding, and refuse to be fooled by it any longer.

The June bug was fooled by the dress on the porch zapper. The dress on the zapper was *light*. The thing inside the dress was *death*. The June bug never figured out the difference, and he never had any reason to.

You have a Bible. You have a reason. Your eternal destiny depends upon it. The Bible has been exposing the bait since Eden. Use it.

Discussion Questions:

1. Read Matthew 4:1-11. Pick one of the three temptations of Jesus and describe how the bait was custom-tied to the situation. What dress was that bait wearing?

2. The chapter says the dangerous thing is dressed up in clothes that look exactly like the safe thing. Have you ever realized after a sin that the bait was wearing a dress? What was the dress, and what was actually inside it?

3. Look back at the five common dresses in the application section: *just one more time*, *I deserve this*, *nobody will get hurt*, *this is just who I am*, and *God will forgive me*. Which one have you used most often on yourself? Why does that particular dress fit you?

4. Read Proverbs 27:20. Why can the bait never actually deliver what it promises? What happens to the lust each time the bait pretends to satisfy it?

5. Jesus answered every piece of bait with a verse of Scripture. What does that tell you about how you ought to be preparing now for the next bait that shows up in your life?

6. Take one piece of bait that has worked on you in the past. What is it dressed as? What is actually inside the dress? Try to write the answer in one honest sentence.

Chapter 6

The Slow Circle

Samson should have known better.

He was a Judge of Israel. He was set apart to God from the womb. The angel of the Lord had appeared to his parents twice before he was born, telling them what their son would be. Manoah and his wife had raised him with that truth, leading him every day of his childhood. He had grown up knowing he was different, and God had used him in ways no other man in Israel had been used in his lifetime. He had killed a lion with his bare hands. He had killed a thousand Philistines with the jawbone of a donkey. He had carried the gates of Gaza on his shoulders up the side of a hill in the dead of night.

Then he met Delilah...

She lived in the valley of Sorek, west of Jerusalem, on the border with the Philistines. The text does not tell us much about how they met or how long they had been together before what we are about to read. It just says Samson loved her. That is all we get for context.

> *"And it came to pass afterward, that he loved a woman in the valley of Sorek, whose name was Delilah"* (Judges 16:4).

The lords of the Philistines came to her in private. They offered her eleven hundred pieces of silver each if she would find out where Samson's strength came from. She agreed. And then she did one of the most patient, ruthless, repetitive things any woman has ever done in the Bible.

She started asking.

> *"Tell me, I pray thee, wherein thy great strength lieth, and wherewith thou mightest be bound to afflict thee."* (Judges 16:6)

She worked to wear him down. Samson lied to her at first. He told her that if they bound him with seven green withs that had not been dried, he would be as weak as any other man. So she sent for the green withs, and he lay down with her, and the Philistine lords came in to take him, and Samson snapped the green withs like burnt thread and got up and walked out.

That should have been the end. It seems that any man with half a brain would have left the valley of Sorek that night and not come back. He surely knew what was happening. The woman was clearly working for the Philistines. The Philistines had been waiting in the next room. The whole evening had been a trap, and he had walked into it with his eyes open.

Yet, Samson came back.

She tried again. *"Surely this time tell me how thou mightest be bound"* (Judges 16:10). He lied to her again. He told her that if they bound him with new ropes that had never been used, he would be as weak as any other man. She bound him, again. The Philistines came again. He snapped the ropes and walked out, again.

He came back a third time.

This time, she added something. She started complaining. She told him he had played her for a fool. *"Hitherto thou hast mocked me, and told me lies"* (Judges 16:13). She turned the whole thing into a question of love. *"How canst thou say, I love thee, when thine heart is not with me?"* (Judges 16:15).

Samson came back a fourth time.

The text says one of the most painful things in the entire chapter:

> *"And it came to pass, when she pressed him daily with her words, and urged him, so that his soul was vexed unto death; that he told her all his heart..."* (Judges 16:16-17)

She pressed him daily. *Daily.* That is the part of the verse that breaks my heart. This was not a single night of weakness. This was a slow, daily wearing-down of a man who kept going back to a woman who was actively trying to destroy him - and he knew it. He could feel her closing the trap. He could see what was happening. He had escaped three times, and the fourth time was already in motion. Yet, he stayed. He lingered.

He told her about the Nazirite vow. He told her the hair was the sign of it, and that if his head were shaved, the strength would leave him.

She lulled him to sleep on her knees. She called for a man to shave the seven locks of his head. The Lord departed from him, and he did not know it. The Philistines took him. They put out his eyes. They bound him with brass fetters. They put him to grinding in the prison house in Gaza, like an ox at a millstone.

He, like the June-bug, had circled Delilah three times. The fourth time, the lap got too tight.

That is the slow circle, and that is what this chapter is about.

There is a very easy-to-overlook section in James 1 that James does not name explicitly, but it is right there in the verse if you know where to look.

> *"But every man is tempted, when he is drawn away of his own lust, and enticed. Then when lust hath conceived, it bringeth forth sin..."* (James 1:14-15)

Notice the small word in the middle of those two verses. *Then.* James does not say *immediately.* He does not say, *and the next thing happens automatically.* He says *then.* The word then has an element of time built into it. That word has a stretch of time in it. The pull and the bait have already met. Something is already moving inside you. But the conception has not happened yet. The line between *being tempted* and *intending to sin* has not been crossed quite yet.

That is perhaps the most dangerous stretch of road in the whole journey. It is the slow circle toward the bug zapper. It is the lap before the final lap of death.

I honestly believe that this is where most Christians lose this battle with sin.

Most Christians try to fight the wrong battle in the wrong place. They think the battle is at stop five, where the act happens, so they walk through stops one, two, three, and four with their guard down. They tell themselves they are fine. They tell themselves they have not actually done anything yet. They tell themselves nothing is really wrong as long as the act has not been committed yet.

The bait was tied on, though. The pull was felt. Something inside them turned. They knew it. They could feel it. They kept walking the same circle they had been walking. The notification was already on the screen, but they had not opened it yet. The conversation was already off-color, but they had not joined in yet. The girl who was not their girlfriend was already on their mind, but they had not texted her yet. The video was already pulled up, but they had not pressed play yet.

Every one of those is a lap. Every lap is a chance to leave. Every lap also makes the next one easier.

That is what the bass was doing in chapter three. That is what the June bug was doing in chapter one. That is what Samson was doing every time he came back to Delilah. He had not given up the Nazirite vow yet. He was lapping the trap, and every time he lapped it, the trap got closer to him.

You have done this. I have done this. We have circled. You have stayed in the room you should have left. You have kept reading the text thread you should have closed.

You have looked one more time at the photo you should not have opened in the first place. You have put off the decision to walk away until you had walked one more lap, and then one more, until you forgot when the laps had started or how many you had taken.

The slow circle is where the pull turns into the fall.

The Hebrew writer warned us about this in plain words.

> *"But exhort one another daily, while it is called To day; lest any of you be hardened through the deceitfulness of sin."* (Hebrews 3:13)

The deceitfulness of sin. That is the phrase. Sin lies to you about how much time you have. Sin lies to you about how much room you have. Sin lies to you about whether you have crossed the line yet or not. Sin tells you, every single time, that you can walk one more lap before you actually have to make a decision. Sin keeps the line just a little bit further out than where you are right now. *I have not crossed the line. I am close to it, but I have not crossed it. I am still in the safe zone.*

The trick is that the line keeps moving with you. Every lap you take moves the line. The slow circle is not measured by where you are, but by where you are going. Samson was not bound and blinded yet when he came back the second time, but he was already on the road to it. He was not bound and blinded yet when he came back the third time, but the trap was tighter than it had been the time before. He was not bound and blinded yet when he started telling her the truth on the fourth visit, but by then, the body was catching up to where the heart had been heading for weeks.

The danger of the slow circle is that you cannot tell exactly where the conception happens. You cannot tell exactly when *I shouldn't* turns into *I want to.* The flip is not loud. The flip is not announced. The flip has happened by the time you notice it has happened. By then, there is nothing left to fight at the heart level. The next move is the act.

Look at how God has tried to help us with this.

In 1 Corinthians 10:13, He says He will always provide a way of escape.

> *"There hath no temptation taken you but such as is common to man: but God is faithful, who will not suffer you to be tempted above that ye are able; but will with the temptation also make a way to escape, that ye may be able to bear it."*

God provides that escape door, but it is yours to walk through. He does not drag you through it the way the angels dragged Lot out of Sodom. He sets it open. He lights it up. He waits to see whether you will turn toward it.

The slow circle is what you do when you walk past the door three times before you finally take it.

The slow circle is what you do when you tell yourself you will leave in five more minutes, and then five more, and then five more.

The slow circle is what you do when the way of escape is right there, and you let yourself stay in the room one more lap because the bait still has its dress on.

The longer you stay, the harder it gets to walk out, because every minute in the room makes the heart a little less able to leave.

Joseph in Genesis 39 did the opposite of the slow circle, and we will spend a whole chapter on him in chapter twelve. For now, just notice what he did. Potiphar's wife came at him *day by day* (Genesis 39:10). Almost the same word as the one used about Delilah. *Daily.* The pressure was constant. She tried to wear Joseph down. The bait was right in front of him, in the same house, day after day, week after week, month after month.

Joseph did not negotiate with her, though. Joseph did not lap the room. Joseph did not see how close he could get without actually doing anything. The text says he *"hearkened not unto her, to lie by her, or to be with her"* (Genesis 39:10). He would not even be in the room with her if he could help it. The day she finally caught him alone and grabbed at him, he ran. He left his coat in her hand and ran out of the house.

That is the opposite of the slow circle. That is a man who knew the only way to win this fight was not to be in the room in the first place. He did not stay to test his strength. He did not stay to see whether he could resist. He did not stay because he loved the rush of being almost-tempted and not-quite-falling. He simply left.

Samson stayed. Joseph ran. The two stories are tremendous examples for us to learn from today.

Application:

The pull on you right now does not have to become a fall. There is a stretch of road between the pull and the fall, and that stretch of road belongs to you. You can use it well or badly. You can take the way of escape that God has provided, or you can lap the trap one more time and tell yourself you have it under control.

Here is the test. It's an honest test. The next time you feel the pull, count how many times you put off leaving the room before you either leave or fall. Count the laps. Count the *just one more minutes.* Count the *I'll close this in a second.* Count the *I'm not actually doing anything.*

If you have lapped the trap three times, the trap is winning, no matter what you tell yourself.

The first lap is the cheapest one to leave. We said this already in chapter three, and it is worth saying again. The second lap is harder. The third lap is harder still. By the fourth lap, you are not really making decisions anymore. You are just doing what the previous laps trained you to do.

Make the first lap the only lap. The minute you feel the pull, the minute the bait shows up, the minute your heart starts moving in a direction it should not move, leave. Do not lap. Do not negotiate. Do not see how strong you are tonight. Walk out of the room. Close the screen. End the conversation. Throw the bottle out. Get up off the couch. Drive the long way home. Do whatever it takes to stop the circling before the lap closes.

You are not weaker than other Christians who do this well. You have just been more willing to lap.

Samson did not have to die in Gaza grinding at a millstone with his eyes put out. Joseph did not have to live the rest of his life with the regret of falling. Neither did. The difference between them was not that Joseph had less lust than Samson. The difference was that Joseph did not lap. He did not stay in the room. He did not test the trap. He left.

The June bug, again, never had this option. He did not have a category for *lap.* He could not say to himself, *I have circled this zapper twice already, and the third time will be the last.* He just kept circling until the contact happened, because circling is all his instinctual wiring lets him do.

You are not wired that way. You have a heart that can be changed and told what to do. You have a mind that can choose. You have a Bible that names the slow circle for what it is, and you have a Lord who has promised you a way of escape every single time the trap closes around you. The way of escape is real. The door is open. You just have to walk through it before the lap is too tight.

That is the goal of the rest of this book. That is what we are about to start learning how to do.

The next chapter goes inside, into the moment of conception itself. The lap closes. The heart yields. *I shouldn't* turns into *I want to.* We have to look at that flip carefully, because if you can see it happening in real time, you can stop the act before it is born.

Discussion Questions:

1. Read Judges 16:6-17. Count how many times Samson came back to Delilah after she had clearly tried to betray him. What does that tell you about the slow circle in your own life?

2. The chapter says the most dangerous stretch of road is between *enticed* and *lust hath conceived.* Why is that stretch so dangerous? Why do most Christians lose right there?

3. Hebrews 3:13 talks about the *deceitfulness of sin.* What does sin lie to you about during the slow circle? What lies have you believed during your own laps?

4. Read 1 Corinthians 10:13. The way of escape is always there. Why do we walk past it so often before we finally take it?

5. Compare Samson and Joseph. Joseph ran on the first lap. Samson stayed for many. What is the actual difference between the two men, in terms of how they handled the slow circle?

6. The chapter says the first lap is the cheapest one to leave. When was the last time you actually left on the first lap? What got you out, and what would have happened if you had lapped one more time?

Chapter 7

Lust Conceived

Cain stood in the field with a stone in his hand, and his brother was standing in front of him.

That is not where the murder started. Unfortunately, that is just where it finished.

The first family in the world had been outside the garden for a long time by the time Cain killed his brother. Adam and Eve had sons. The sons had grown. Cain worked the ground and grew crops. Abel kept sheep. They had both been raised on the story of the garden, on the story of the serpent, on the story of why their parents could not go back home. They surely had been told what God expected of them. They had been taught how to bring an offering. They had grown up with the family altar, the family memory, and the family hope. They knew who God was and what He required.

The day came when both brothers brought offerings to the Lord. Abel brought a lamb from the firstlings of his flock. Cain brought some of the fruit of the ground. The Lord had respect for Abel and for his offering. He did not respect Cain or his offering. The Bible does not give us the long version of why. It just tells us what happened in Cain's face.

"And Cain was very wroth, and his countenance fell." (Genesis 4:5)

But we are not left completely in the dark. The Bible itself tells us elsewhere what made the difference.

> *"By faith Abel offered unto God a more excellent sacrifice than Cain, by which he obtained witness that he was righteous, God testifying of his gifts."* (Hebrews 11:4)

Abel brought his lamb by faith. Cain brought his fruit some other way. That is what separated them in God's sight. Not the work in the field. Not the sweat on the brow. The faith behind the offering.

Now stack that next to what Paul wrote to the Romans.

> *"So then faith cometh by hearing, and hearing by the word of God."* (Romans 10:17)

Faith does not come out of thin air. It does not rise out of a man's own thinking. It comes by hearing the word of God. If Abel offered by faith, then Abel had heard. And if Abel had heard, Cain had heard the same thing. They were brothers. They grew up under the same roof, around the same altar, learning from the same father. God had spoken. They both knew what He expected. Abel obeyed it. Cain decided he had a better idea.

His face fell. He glared at the ground. Something inside him went red hot. He was the firstborn, and his younger brother had just been preferred over him in front of God. He had also made an offering to God. The fury rose in his chest, and he did not put it down.

This moment is where the chapter we are about to open really begins. Not in the field with the stone. Here. In Cain's chest, with the heat rising and his face falling, and his offering on the altar behind him.

God spoke to him then. He did not wait for the murder. He stepped in early, the way a Father will, and He warned His son.

> *"And the LORD said unto Cain, Why art thou wroth? and why is thy countenance fallen? If thou doest well, shalt thou not be accepted? and if thou doest not well, sin lieth at the door. And unto thee shall be his desire, and thou shalt rule over him." (*Genesis 4:6-7)

Read those words slowly. The murder has not happened yet. Abel is still alive. He is somewhere out with his sheep, doing what shepherds do. But God describes the sin as if it were already a creature, crouched at the doorway of Cain's heart, breathing, waiting to be let in. Sin was not far away. Sin was right there at the threshold, and the only thing keeping it out was Cain's willingness to keep saying no.

God says one more thing. *Unto thee shall be his desire, and thou shalt rule over him.* Sin wanted Cain. Sin was reaching for him the same way Cain wanted to reach for what he had no right to. The question was who would rule over whom.

Cain did not rule over it.

The next verse, the very next verse in the Bible, says,

> *"And Cain talked with Abel his brother: and it came to pass, when they were in the field, that Cain rose up against Abel his brother, and slew him"* (Genesis 4:8).

Look at the sequence. Cain talked with Abel. Cain led Abel out into the field. Cain rose up. Cain slew Abel. By the time the stone came down, the murder had already been finished in the heart of the man holding the stone. The act in the field was the body doing what the heart had already decided.

Abel did not die in the field. Abel died in his brother's mind and heart first. The field was just where the body caught up.

Lust Conceived

That is the next stop on James's road. That is what James calls *lust hath conceived.*

"Then when lust hath conceived, it bringeth forth sin..."(James 1:15a)

The Greek word James uses for *conceived* is *syllambanō*. It is a compound word built from *syn* (together) and *lambanō*(to take or receive). Literally, to take together. To grasp. To seize. To take hold of. The word is used several times in the New Testament to describe a woman becoming pregnant. When two things meet within her body, a new life begins. It is the word the angel uses with Mary in Luke 1:31, when he tells her she will conceive in her womb and bring forth a son. It is the word Elizabeth uses about herself in Luke 1:36. It is a real, biological, life-starting word.

That is the picture that James is drawing for us. The lust on the inside meets the bait on the outside. They take hold of each other. They grasp each other. The two come together, and something new is conceived. From the moment of that conception forward, a sin has begun its life inside you. Unless something interrupts it, the sin will grow until it is born into the world as an act.

The conception is invisible from the outside. Nobody watching Cain in the moments after his offering was rejected would have known what was happening in him. He still looked like a farmer. He still had a face and hands. The fury rising in him was not yet a body in the field. But the deepest part of him had already shifted. The yes had been given. From that moment, the next chapter of his life was already written. The murder was on the way.

The conception is the sin. The act is the announcement.

This point is where Jesus took his hardest line on the inner life. He went on the record about it on a hillside in Galilee, in front of crowds of ordinary people who had been raised on the Ten Commandments their whole lives. He did not soften the commandments. He went deeper than the commandments. He took the laws against murder and adultery and traced them back to the heart, where conception happens.

> *"Ye have heard that it was said by them of old time, Thou shalt not kill; and whosoever shall kill shall be in danger of the judgment: But I say unto you, That whosoever is angry with his brother without a cause shall be in danger of the judgment..."* (Matthew 5:21-22)

He said it again about adultery a few verses later.

> *"Ye have heard that it was said by them of old time, Thou shalt not commit adultery: But I say unto you, That whosoever looketh on a woman to lust after her hath committed adultery with her already in his heart."* (Matthew 5:27-28)

Read those with James in your other ear. Jesus and James are saying the same thing. The act is downstream of the conception in the heart. By the time the body acts, the spiritual sin has already been committed in the inner room of the soul. The act is not where the sin starts. The act is where the sin shows its face. The sin happened upstream, when the looking became wanting, when the wanting became yielding, when the lust conceived.

The same is true of every sin. Murder happens in the heart before it happens in the field. Adultery happens in the heart before it happens in the bed. Theft starts in the heart before it reaches the cash drawer. Slander happens in the heart before it ever leaves the mouth. The body is the messenger. The conception is the sin.

John takes this teaching one step further to show you how serious it is.

> *"Whosoever hateth his brother is a murderer: and ye know that no murderer hath eternal life abiding in him."* (1 John 3:15)

Read that slowly. John says hatred in the heart is murder. Not *leads to murder*. Not *is dangerous like murder*. Is murder. The conception is already the act, in God's eyes. The body has not killed anybody yet, and the body does not have to. The killing happened upstream, the same place Cain's killing of Abel happened, hours before the stone ever came down.

If you have ever wondered why God takes sin as seriously as He does, this is part of it. He sees what the body has not yet done, but the heart has already conceived. He does not have to wait for the act. He saw the conception.

Fighting Conception

So, how do you fight all of this at the conception point?

This is the hardest stop on James's road, because nothing has happened yet that anybody can point to. There is no act. There is no body in the field. There is no scene anybody else could see. There is only what is happening inside you. The fight has gotten so quiet that it almost cannot be fought.

Solomon writes the line everybody quotes about the heart. Most people quote half of it. The whole verse is what matters.

> *"Keep thy heart with all diligence; for out of it are the issues of life."* (Proverbs 4:23)

Keep your heart. Guard it. With all diligence, which means with everything you have, all the time, with both eyes open. Why? Because every river of your life flows out of that one spring. What you do, what you say, what you become, what you fail to become, all of it comes from the heart. The act is downstream. The conception is upstream. If you guard the spring, you guard the whole river.

What does guarding the heart look like at the conception stage?

It looks like watching for the moment of yielding. It looks like catching the inner shift before the body executes it. It looks like refusing to let the wrestling stop. It looks like keeping the doorway closed when sin is crouching at the threshold, as

God told Cain to do. It looks like saying out loud, in the inner room, the sentence Cain refused to say. *No. Not today. Not ever. Get back from the door.*

You will not always succeed at this. Nobody does, except the Lord. But you will start succeeding more often the day you start watching for the conception. Most Christians have no category for this stage. They think the only thing they have to fight is the act. They walk through the conception with their eyes closed, telling themselves nothing is happening, and wake up in the field with the stone in their hand, unable to figure out how they got there.

My goal is to teach you to keep your eyes open at the door.

Here is something hard for most to understand, but the truth of it can help. The moment of conception almost always feels like relief. Watch for the relief.

The wrestling has been hard. The praying has been hard. The fight has been hard. And then, somewhere in the middle of it, the fight goes quiet. You feel calm. You feel settled. You feel like the conflict is over. That feeling is not always the peace of God. That feeling can also be the conception. The peace of God does not come from simply stopping the wrestling. It comes from the wrestling being won.

If the wrestling stops because you have laid the lust at the foot of the cross and turned your eyes to Christ, you will know it. There will be a clean stillness, a quiet that goes the right way, a sense that something has been settled in the direction of the Lord. If the wrestling stops because the inner yes has been given to the lust, you will feel calm too, but the calm will go the wrong way. You will feel relieved that the fight is over, and within a few minutes, you will find yourself reaching for the thing you swore you would not reach for.

The two kinds of relief are not hard to tell apart if you stop and ask the right question. Where is your heart pointed right now? Toward the Lord, or toward the bait? The answer to that question tells you which kind of quiet has just settled on you.

Most of the time, we do not stop to ask. So the wrestling goes quiet, the relief washes over, and we end up doing the thing we hate. Watch for the relief. Watch where it is pointing you.

There is something else worth saying about the conception, and it is the way the inner yes usually puts itself into words.

The inner yes does not come dressed as rebellion. It does not come with loud thunder and fire from Heaven. It almost always comes wearing the clothes of a small, quiet sentence. The same handful of sentences show up over and over again across every kind of sin and every kind of believer. If you can recognize them when they show up in your own head, you can sometimes catch the conception before it finishes.

This time will be different. That is one of the most common ones. You have probably been saying that to yourself for years. You have not been right yet. You will not be right tomorrow either. The moment that sentence shows up in your head, you can be sure you are very close to the doorway.

I can stop whenever I want. That sentence is incorrect and misstates who is in charge. The lust is in charge in that moment, not you. If you could stop, you would have stopped already.

It is not really that bad. That sentence shrinks the sin so it can fit through the door. The sin will not stay shrunk once it is inside.

God knows my heart. That sentence twists a true statement into an excuse. God does know your heart. That is exactly the problem. He sees the conception coming before the act is born, and the sentence that uses His knowledge to permit oneself is one of the most dangerous sentences a Christian can say.

I will deal with this later. That sentence pushes the wrestling into the future and yields the present. There is no later. There is only now. The conception happens in the now; you keep refusing to fight in. In Cameroon, there is a hymn that says, "Tomorrow is right now." We should maybe live more like that instead of denying the truth.

When any of those sentences show up in the inner room, you are at the doorway. The sentences are not the conception itself, but they are the words the conception almost always speaks just before it happens. Hear them, name them, and refuse to keep listening. Walk back into the wrestling.

You Can Stop It Still

There is one more thing to say before we close.

The conception can be interrupted, even at very late stages.

The Bible is full of men and women who walked right up to the edge of the inner yes and turned back. Joseph in Egypt turned back. Daniel in Babylon turned back. Esther in Persia turned back. Job on the ash heap turned back when his wife told him to curse God and die. The Lord Jesus in the wilderness turned back three times in a row in front of the tempter himself. Every one of them stood in the doorway with sin crouching at the threshold. Everyone of them looked at the doorway and said no.

You can do that too. You will not always do it. You will fail some of the time, as every Christian who has ever lived has. But you will do it more than you used to do it the day you start watching for the doorway at all. And when you fail, the blood of Christ is enough to wash you and put you back on the road.

"If we confess our sins, he is faithful and just to forgive us our sins, and to cleanse us from all unrighteousness" (1 John 1:9).

The conception that gets confessed is the conception that does not have to be born.

The June-bug never had this fight. He had no inner room. He had no heart to guard. He flew at the light because that was all he was. You are not all you are, like an animal or insect. You have a heart that can be guarded. You have a Word that names what is happening inside that heart. You have a Lord who has stood at the doorway of every conception you will ever face and walked away without yielding once.

Lean on Him. Watch your inner room. Keep the wrestling going.

The conception is invisible. The conception is also stoppable. Both are true at the same time.

Discussion Questions:

1. Read Genesis 4:1-8 again. The murder of Abel happened in the field. However, the chapter argues that the conception happened in Cain's heart while his offering was still smoking. Why does the order matter? What does it teach you about your own anger?

2. God told Cain that *"sin lieth at the door"* before the murder ever happened. Have you ever felt sin crouching at a doorway in your own heart? What did it look like? What kept the door closed, or what opened it?

3. In Matthew 5:27-28, Jesus says adultery in the heart is already adultery. In 1 John 3:15, John says hatred in the heart is murder. Why does God count what the body has not yet done? What does this teach you about the depth of His knowledge of you?

4. Read Proverbs 4:23. What would it look like for you to *keep your heart with all diligence* this week? Name one specific way.

5. The chapter says the moment of conception almost always feels like relief, the wrestling going suddenly quiet. How is the relief of conception different from the peace of God? Have you ever felt the wrong kind of relief and missed it for the right kind?

6. The chapter ends by saying the conception is stoppable, even very late. What is one conception you can feel coming this week? What would it look like to interrupt it before the act is born?

Chapter 8

Sin Born

David should have been at war.

The text of 2 Samuel 11 makes this point in the very first verse, almost before the story has a chance to start.

> *"And it came to pass, after the year was expired, at the time when kings go forth to battle, that David sent Joab, and his servants with him, and all Israel; and they destroyed the children of Ammon, and besieged Rabbah. But David tarried still at Jerusalem."* (2 Samuel 11:1)

It is the kind of opening line a writer uses when he wants you to feel something heavy before the story has even started. *At the time when kings go forth to battle.* That is what the king of Israel was supposed to be doing in the spring of that year. Joab was out there. The army was out there. The men of Israel were out there. Yet, the king of Israel was on a rooftop in Jerusalem.

He could not sleep. The text says he had risen from his bed in the evening, which seems to be the language of a man who had napped during the day, restless, getting up to wander on the flat roof of his palace as the sun was going down. From the roof of the king's house, he could see down into the courtyards of the houses below. The terraced architecture of Jerusalem made that possible. A king on a high roof could look down into the lives of his subjects.

That night, he saw a woman bathing.

The text does not blame Bathsheba for the bath. The text does not indicate that she was trying to be seen. She was washing herself in a private courtyard, performing a ritual cleansing required by the law of Moses, in a place where she had every reasonable right to expect privacy. The man on the high roof was the problem. He was the one whose eye lingered. He was the one who turned his head a quarter inch and then a quarter inch more.

Then the conception happened. That flip that we talked about in the last chapter. Somewhere on that roof, in the seconds between *I see her* and *I am going to do something about her*, David's heart yielded. The wrestling, if there had been any, went quiet. He stopped seeing the woman as a sister in Israel and began seeing her as something he would take.

Then he sent for her.

Read those four words again, because there is a whole chapter packed into them. *He sent for her.* That is the act of being born. That is the conception turning into the deed. That is the moment when what had been alive in his head walked out into the world. Servants were dispatched. They went to the woman's house. They knocked on the door. They told her the king was asking for her. She came. He took her. She conceived a literal child in her womb. The act produced its own conception, in the most literal sense the Bible ever uses that word.

The whole chain of events is there in two verses.

> *"And David sent and inquired after the woman... And David sent messengers, and took her; and she came in unto him, and he lay with her..."* (2 Samuel 11:3-4)

That is a picture of the Greek word *tiktō.* That is the verb James uses when he says *"lust, when it hath conceived, bringeth forth sin"* (James 1:15). *Tiktō* is the Greek word for giving birth. It is what a mother does at the end of nine months.

It is what a chicken does when she lays an egg. It is what a tree does when an apple finally drops off the branch. Whatever has been growing inside finally comes out. The hidden thing becomes visible. The private becomes the public. The conception becomes the child.

What was alive in David's heart on the roof was now alive in his bedroom. The sin had been born.

This is the stop most people think of when they think of sin. This is the visible part—the actual act. The thing that somebody else can catch you in. The thing you end up confessing. The thing you regret. The thing we associate with the consequences of our actions. The thing that wakes you up at three o'clock in the morning, a week later, with a knot in your stomach.

But notice where it sits in the road.

Source. Pull. Bait. Conception. Birth.

The act is fifth. By the time the act is born, four other things have already happened. Four other places where the chain could have been broken existed. Four other stops on the road got walked through with the guard down. The act is just the last one. The act is just the part the world sees.

That is not how most of us were taught about sin. Most of us were taught that the act is everything. Don't drink. Don't sleep with her. Don't lie. Don't steal. Don't hit your sister. The whole moral framework we were taught in our childhood was built around behaviors. Stay away from those behaviors, and you are doing well. Commit those behaviors, and you are doing poorly. In our minds, the whole architecture of the Christian life was about managing actions.

James says by the time you are looking at the act, you have already lost four prior battles. The actions are very real and countable. The actions matter eternally. But the final actions are not where the war is fought. The actions are actually where the war ends.

David lost the war on the roof. The war was not lost in the bedroom. By the time he was in the bedroom, all the losing was already over.

Look at what the act actually does once it is born.

The Lie

The first thing it does is it lies to you about itself. The bait that brought you to the act told you it would feel a certain way. *Just one more time. Nobody will get hurt. You will feel better afterward.* The act does not deliver. The act **never**delivers. The act gives you about thirty seconds of what the bait promised, and then the rest of it is something you did not expect. The video does not actually feel the way you thought it would by the time you close the screen. The drink does not actually warm you the way you thought it would by the time the bottle is empty. The angry words do not actually relieve the pressure the way you thought they would by the time your wife is in tears in the other room.

The Lord said this through Jeremiah eight hundred years before James wrote his letter:

"For my people have committed two evils; they have forsaken me, the fountain of living waters, and hewed them out cisterns, broken cisterns, that can hold no water." (Jeremiah 2:13)

Read that verse again very carefully. A fountain of living waters means a spring that bubbles up out of the ground on its own and never stops. It does not need to be filled. It does not need to be maintained. It just keeps giving, and giving, and giving, because the source is underneath it. A cistern is a hole carved out of the rock that you have to fill yourself. A cistern is not a source. A cistern is a container. And a cracked cistern is not even that. A cracked cistern is a hole you fill, and the water leaks out of, and you have to keep filling, and it never holds anything for long.

That is what every sinful act is. A cracked cistern. You hew it out of the rock with your own hands. You climb down into it expecting to find water. The water leaks out before you can drink it. You climb back up thirsty. Then you hew another one. Then another. Then another. Your whole life can be spent digging cisterns that do not hold water, when there was a spring of living water flowing the whole time you were digging.

The act always promises what it cannot deliver. The act always lies. That is what makes it a sin in the first place.

The Change

The second thing the act does is it changes you.

The man who walks out of the room after the act is not the same man who walked in. Something has shifted. The Bible talks about this in language that should make you sit up and take notice. Romans 6 says you become a slave to whatever you obey. "

Know ye not, that to whom ye yield yourselves servants to obey, his servants ye are to whom ye obey"(Romans 6:16).

Every act of sin is a small act of yielding. Every yielding builds a path. Every path gets deeper the more you walk on it. Eventually, the track becomes a rut. Eventually, the rut becomes a chain of slavery to sin.

That is why the same sin keeps showing up in your life. That is why the same act keeps being born out of the same lust through the same bait. You did not just commit an act last time. You laid down a pathway. The next time the bait shows up, the pathway is already there, and your foot finds it without thinking because it is familiar and easy. The act is born faster the second time. Faster the third. Faster the fourth.

This is also why sin escalates. The track does not just get deeper. It gets wider. It needs more. The first drink could not stay just one. The first angry word could not stay quiet. The act, once born, is not satisfied to be born again the same size. It wants to grow.

David's act of taking another man's wife did not remain an act of taking another man's wife. By the end of the same chapter, it had grown into the murder of Uriah the Hittite, one of David's own most loyal soldiers, killed by being placed in the hottest part of the battle and then deliberately abandoned there. David became a murderer because he had first become an adulterer. The act of adultery would not stay adultery. It needed a cover. It needed to keep itself hidden. So it grew up into murder, the way every act of sin will grow up into something larger if you give it the chance.

The Leak

The third thing the act does is it leaks.

We will spend more time on this in the next chapter, when we talk about the death that sin gives birth to. But it has to be said here too, because it sits inside the act itself. There is no such thing as a truly private sin, even when done in true privacy. There is no such thing as an act that affects only the person who commits it. Every act of sin leaks into the lives of the people around the sinner.

David's act on the roof leaked into Bathsheba's life. It leaked into Uriah's life, which lasted only a few weeks longer because of it. It leaked into the life of the child she carried, who died seven days after birth. It leaked into the life of the prophet Nathan, who had to walk into the king's chamber and tell him a parable about a stolen sheep, only to watch the king condemn himself with his own mouth. It leaked into the life of David's older son, Amnon, who would later force himself on his half-sister Tamar in a sin that looked very much like his father's. It leaked into the life of David's son Absalom, who would eventually rebel against his father and try to take the throne. It leaked into the life of the entire kingdom of Israel.

One act on a roof: a whole kingdom, generations of family, a child in a cradle. The act leaked.

Yours leaks too. Whatever sinful act you walked away from this past month, thinking *that was a private thing, nobody saw it, nobody got hurt*, has already started leaking into the people around you. They will not always know what changed in you. They will feel that something has changed. They will feel a coldness, or a distance, or a quickness of temper, or a subtle shift in the way you talk to them. The act has begun to do its work in them, even if they cannot name it. The act always leaks.

Application:

The next time you are about to commit a sinful act, before you do it, do this one thing. Look at the act for what it actually is. Expose it the way we did with the bait in chapter five. Name it.

It is not *just looking at this one video.* It is opening a doorway in your soul that you have been trying to close, inviting the lust back in for another round, and adding another notch to a track that goes back further than you want to admit.

It is not *just one drink with the guys.* It is renewing a relationship with alcohol that has already cost you more than you can afford to lose, and pretending the next drink will somehow be different from the last ones.

It is not *just blowing up at her one time because she pushed me.* It is teaching the woman God gave you that your love is conditional on her being easy to live with, and teaching your children that fathers respond to stress with loud voices.

The act is what it is. Strip the dress. Look at it. Then decide whether you still want to give birth to it.

The conception has happened, but the birth has not. There is still a small window between *I want to* and *I did.* You can interrupt the act after conception and before birth. It is harder than interrupting at any of the earlier stops. It is not impossible. The God who has provided a way of escape at every other stop has not abandoned you at this one. The door is still open. The escape is still there. The act does not have to be born tonight.

But you have to be willing to look at the act for what it actually is, instead of for what the bait is still trying to dress it up as. The bait does not stop dressing the act just because the conception is over. The bait keeps dressing the entire way through.

The June-bug never had to look at his act for what it was. The June-bug never had a category for *act*. The contact with the zapper happened to him, and he was gone, and there was no consciousness left in him to evaluate what had happened or what would happen next. You are not the June-bug. You can stop. You can look. You can name. You can refuse.

Use the room God gave you between the conception and the birth. Use it tonight.

For Discussion

1. Read 2 Samuel 11:1-4. The first verse points out that David should have been at war. What does it mean to be in a place you should not be when the bait shows up? How does location set the table for the act?

2. The chapter says the act is fifth on the road, not first. How has it changed your understanding of sin to see the act as the end of a chain rather than the beginning?

3. Read Jeremiah 2:13. The act always promises what it cannot deliver. What sins in your life have been broken cisterns, holes you keep digging that never hold water?

4. Read Romans 6:16. Every act of sin lays down a track. What tracks have you laid down over the years, and what would it take to stop deepening them?

5. The author says there is no such thing as a private sin, because every act leaks. Where has a "private" sin of yours actually leaked into other people's lives? What did the leak look like?

6. There is a small window between conception and birth where the act can still be interrupted. What practical step could you take during that window to give yourself a chance to walk away?

Chapter 9

Death Finished

David thought he had gotten away with it.

It had been almost a year. Bathsheba was now his wife, brought into the palace after the prescribed period of mourning for her husband, Uriah. The child she had been carrying when David first took her was about to be born. The men in the army had moved on. Joab had kept his mouth shut. The servants who had carried the messages had kept their mouths shut. The whole episode was buried under the weight of palace business, royal duties, and the slow grind of months passing without anybody calling the king to account.

Then a man named Nathan walked into the throne room.

Nathan was a prophet of the Lord, and he had been one of David's friends. He came to the king with a story. He said there were two men in a certain city. One was rich, with great flocks and herds. The other was poor and had nothing in the world but one little ewe lamb. He had bought it. He had raised it. The lamb ate from his table and drank from his cup and slept in his arms, the text says, like a daughter to him.

A traveler came to the rich man's house. The rich man, instead of taking from his own flocks to feed his guest, sent his servants out to take the poor man's lamb. They killed it, dressed it, and served it to the visitor on a platter.

David's blood went hot.

> *"And David's anger was greatly kindled against the man; and he said to Nathan, As the Lord liveth, the man that hath done this thing shall surely die: And he shall restore the lamb fourfold, because he did this thing, and because he had no pity."* (2 Samuel 12:5-6)

That is when Nathan turned. The prophet looked his king in the face and said four words that you and I have to hear over and over again until they sink into our bones.

> *"And Nathan said to David, Thou art the man."* (2 Samuel 12:7)

David's act was done. The conception was a year old. The birth was a year old. He had assumed the road ended in his bedroom, that the act itself was the end of the chain, that everything afterward would be ordinary life with the sin tucked away in a drawer behind him.

It does not work like that.

Nathan kept talking. The Lord, through his prophet, told David what was coming next. The sword would never depart from his house. His own family would rise against him from inside his own walls. His wives would be taken in broad daylight. The child Bathsheba was carrying would die. The peace David thought he had purchased with the cover-up was a peace that had never existed. The road still had stops on it that David had not yet seen.

And every one of those stops came true.

The child died seven days after birth. David's daughter Tamar was raped by his oldest son Amnon, who was then murdered by his other son Absalom in revenge. Absalom rebelled against his father, drove him out of Jerusalem, slept publicly with David's concubines on the roof of the palace where the whole story had started, and was eventually killed in the forest of Ephraim, hanging by his hair from an oak tree. David spent his last years as a broken man, watching his sons tear each other apart and listening to news from the front lines that always seemed bad. He died old and full of days, but his house never recovered the way it had been.

That is what James means by *finished.*

> *"Then when lust hath conceived, it bringeth forth sin: and sin, when it is finished, bringeth forth death."* (James 1:15)

The Greek word is *apoteleō.* It means to bring to completion, to finish off, to carry through to the end. James is not talking about the act here. He is past the act. He is past the conception. He is talking about what happens when sin is allowed to mature, to grow up, to run its full course in a person's life. James says when that happens, sin is not done having children. Sin gives birth one more time. And what sin gives birth to at the end of the road is death.

That is the last stop. That is where the road ends.

Most Christians have a hard time taking this step seriously because they think they have already seen it work out. They look at their own life. They have committed sins. They have walked through the conception and the birth more times than they would like to admit. And they are still here. They have not died. The roof has not fallen in on them. They got up the next morning, ate breakfast, went to work, and life went on.

So when James says *death*, they hear it as a metaphor. They hear it as a vague, distant, religious word that does not quite map onto anything they have actually experienced. The act feels like the worst part. The death feels theoretical.

It is not theoretical.

It is just slower than the act. It just shows up later. It just takes longer to grow up than the act took. The act is a baby. Death is the adult that the baby grows into. You have not seen the death yet because you have not let the sin run all the way to the end of the road yet, or you have, and you are not willing to call what you are looking at by its right name.

Death has more than one shape. We need to see them.

Relational Death

The first kind of death sin gives birth to is relational death.

Sin kills relationships. Always. This is the death you can usually see first, because it shows up in real time in the people around you. The marriage that used to work no longer does, and you both know why, even if neither of you will say it out loud. The close friendship has gone cold because something you did changed how your friend looks at you. The relationship between you and your dad has been distant for years, and somewhere underneath the distance is a sin one of you committed against the other and never repented of.

David's relationships died one by one after Bathsheba. His relationship with the Lord went through a long, dark valley that produced Psalms 51 and 32, but never quite recovered the easy intimacy of the years before. His relationship with his sons was poisoned. His relationship with the men who had served him faithfully, such as Joab, grew complicated and cold. The man who had once been the friend of the Lord and the captain of a band of mighty men became the lonely king watching his family fall apart.

Your sin is killing relationships you have not even noticed yet. The killing is slow. It is sometimes silent. But it is happening. The wife who is harder to reach this year than last. The kids who are quieter around you than they used to be. The friend at church who has stopped initiating. None of those things just happens. There is a death working in the middle of them.

Emotional Death

The second kind of death sin gives birth to is emotional death.

This is the death that happens inside you. The thing that used to give you joy no longer does. The Bible that used to feel alive feels like a phone book. The worship that used to lift you off the ground sits on you like a wet blanket. The prayer life that used to be a conversation has become a script you mumble and forget. Something inside you has gone numb. You can feel that you used to feel things. You cannot remember exactly when you stopped.

Solomon went through this the hard way. The wisest man who ever lived walked into a season where he could write the whole book of Ecclesiastes and call everything under the sun *vanity*. Read it carefully, and you can see the hand of sin in it. Solomon had taken seven hundred wives and three hundred concubines, against the explicit command of God to the kings of Israel. The text says that *"his wives turned away his heart"* (1 Kings 11:3). The man who had built the temple, who had received wisdom directly from God, who the Queen of Sheba had visited, ended his life as a man who could find no joy in any of it. The lust had finished its work. The death had been born.

You can feel this in yourself if you are honest. The sin you are committing is dulling something inside you. You are not as moved by the things you used to be. The things that used to scare you no longer do. The things that used to delight you do not delight you anymore. You are slowly being hollowed out, and the sin is doing the hollowing.

Spiritual Death

The third kind of death sin gives birth to is spiritual death.

This is the most dangerous kind, because it is the hardest to see in the mirror. The Lord said through Isaiah that sin separates a man from his God, and that when the separation happens, the heavens themselves seem to go silent.

> *"Behold, the Lord's hand is not shortened, that it cannot save; neither his ear heavy, that it cannot hear: But your iniquities have separated between you and your God, and your sins have hid his face from you, that he will not hear."* (Isaiah 59:1-2)

Sin builds a wall. The wall is not on God's side. God is still where He was. The wall is on your side. The wall is built brick by brick out of every act of sin you commit and refuse to repent of, and the longer the wall stands, the harder it is to hear the voice of the Lord on the other side of it. You do not stop being able to pray. You stop hearing yourself getting answers. You do not stop reading. You stop seeing anything when you read. The Word is still alive. You have just been growing dull to it, one sin at a time.

In the worst cases, this kind of death ends in what the Hebrew writer calls a hardened heart.

> *"But exhort one another daily, while it is called To day; lest any of you be hardened through the deceitfulness of sin"* (Hebrews 3:13).

A hardened heart is a heart that has gone past the point of being moved. It can hear the gospel and feel nothing. It can read about the cross and shrug. It is not unbelief, exactly. It is a numbness that eventually becomes indistinguishable from unbelief. People who are this far gone do not always know they are. They sit in pews. They go through motions. The sin has finished its work.

Literal Death

The fourth kind of death sin gives birth to is the literal one.

> *"For the wages of sin is death; but the gift of God is eternal life through Jesus Christ our Lord."* (Romans 6:23)

That verse is on a thousand church bulletin boards. We have read it so many times that we have stopped hearing it. Read it once more. *The wages of sin is death.* That is what God owes you in exchange for the labor you have put in. The sin has been your work. Death is your paycheck.

The death Paul is talking about in Romans 6 is not just the funeral that ends every human life. It is the second death. It is the death described in Revelation 21:8. This lake burneth with fire and brimstone, where the unbelieving and the murderers and the whoremongers and the sorcerers and the idolaters and all liars have their part. It is eternal separation from God in a place of conscious torment. It is the worst thing the universe contains.

Sin has been growing toward that, in every person who has ever sinned, since the moment the lust was first conceived in the heart. The act is the baby. The death is the adult. Eternal death is what the adult becomes if no one intervenes.

The whole of the New Testament has been written so that no one will have to face that. The whole of the cross has been built so that no one will have to face that. But the death is real, and the only way to make sense of the cross is to take the death seriously enough that you can understand why God's only son had to die in your place.

Galatians says it as a farming metaphor.

> *"Be not deceived; God is not mocked: for whatsoever a man soweth, that shall he also reap. For he that soweth to his flesh shall of the flesh reap corruption; but he that soweth to the Spirit shall of the Spirit reap life everlasting."* (Galatians 6:7-8)

You are sowing right now. Every day of your life is a day of seed-throwing. Every act of sin is a seed in the ground. Every act of obedience is a seed in the ground. The harvest is delayed. That is one of the cruelest deceptions of sin, that the harvest is delayed long enough for you to forget what you planted. By the time the corruption is coming up out of the ground, you cannot always remember which season it was that you put it there. But it grows, the way every seed grows. It grows on God's timetable, not yours.

This is why young people get fooled. The seeds you are planting in your teens and twenties are not going to come up tomorrow. The harvest of sexual sin in college might not be reaped until you're well into your marriage in your mid-thirties. The harvest of pride in your high school years might not be reaped until you are passed over for the third promotion in a row. The harvest of bitterness toward your father might not be reaped until you have a son of your own and cannot figure out why he is afraid of you. The seed always reaps. The harvest is just slow.

This is also why older people get sober. They have lived long enough to see the harvest of seeds they planted decades earlier. The brother in the third pew who sits very quietly during the invitation song is not just being polite. He is remembering things he did when he was your age, and watching the harvest of those things still ripening in his children and grandchildren. He could tell you stories that would change the way you think about this week.

Listen to those men. Sit with those men. Their faces are the future face of every young person who refuses to take the death stop seriously.

Changing Direction

Here is the turn. Here is where the book changes direction.

The first nine chapters of this book have been the diagnosis. We have walked the road. We have seen where it starts, bends, accelerates, and ends. We have looked at the source, the pull, the bait, the conception, the birth, and the death. The road runs in one direction, and the direction is downward, and the bottom is darker than most people are willing to think about.

That is the bad news. The good news is that there is another road, and that road runs the other way. The good news is that everything James describes in three verses, the cross undoes in three days. *"For the wages of sin is death; but the gift of God is eternal life through Jesus Christ our Lord."*

Sin pays a wage. Christ gives a gift.

You cannot earn the gift. That is what makes it a gift. You can only receive it, and you can only receive it on God's terms, in God's way, through faith in His Son who died and rose again, who calls every sinner to repentance and to baptism into His death, that we might walk in newness of life (Romans 6:3-4). The death of Christ has answered the whole death of sin. The resurrection of Christ has answered the whole life of sin. The whole road from conception to death has been swallowed up in His road from the cross to the empty tomb.

The next four chapters of this book will not be more diagnoses. They will be the cure. We have to learn to fight at every stop on the road we just walked, and we have to learn to walk on the new road instead. That is what is coming.

The first half of the book has shown you why you cannot save yourself. The second half of the book shows you how the Lord does it.

Before you turn the page, sit with the death stop one more time. Look at where the road ends if you do not turn around. Look at the kinds of death your sin is already producing in your relationships, in your emotions, in your spirit, and in your eternity. None of those deaths is fixed yet. None of those deaths is final. But every one of them is real, and every one of them is growing in you while you read this.

The June bug is dead because the June bug had no Bible and no Savior. You are not the June bug. The Bible is in your hand. The Savior is on the throne. The death does not have to finish. The road can be turned around right now.

That is what we will do for the rest of this book.

For Discussion

1. Read 2 Samuel 12:1-14. David thought his sin was over when the act was done. What did Nathan reveal about how far the road actually went? What stops on the road did David not yet see?

2. The chapter names four kinds of death that sin gives birth to: relational, emotional, spiritual, and eternal. Which one have you seen most clearly at work in your own life? Which one frightens you the most?

3. Read Isaiah 59:1-2. The wall that separates a sinner from God is on which side, and who builds it? What does that mean for how you ought to handle unconfessed sin?

4. Read Galatians 6:7-8 and the section on the slow harvest. What seeds are you planting right now that you might be reaping in twenty years? Be honest.

5. The chapter says young people get fooled because the harvest is delayed. Why is it harder to take the death stop seriously when you are young? What can you do now to take it seriously anyway?

6. Read Romans 6:23 once more. The wage is death. The gift is eternal life. How does seeing the road of sin end in death change the way you read the gospel?

Chapter 10

See It Coming

There were watchmen in the cities of Israel.

You forget about them when you read the Old Testament, because they show up only in passing. Still, they were essential to a city's survival. Every walled town had a tower over the gate, and every tower had a man on it during every hour of the day and every hour of the night. The watchman's job was simple. He watched the road. He watched the horizon. He watched the country around the city. When something approached the city, the watchman's job was to spot it before anyone else and sound the alarm.

The book of Ezekiel has the Lord giving Ezekiel his commission as a prophet by comparing him to one of these men:

> *"Son of man, I have made thee a watchman unto the house of Israel: therefore hear the word at my mouth, and give them warning from me."* (Ezekiel 33:7)

A watchman who slept on the job would lose his city. A watchman who could not tell the dust of an approaching army from the dust of returning shepherds would either spread panic or miss the attack. A watchman who did not know the faces of the people who lived in the country around his town would let an enemy slip in dressed as a friend. The whole city's safety, in a real sense, hung in the eyes of one tired man on a high tower.

You are that tired man on the high tower. Your soul is the city.

The first half of this book diagnosed the disease of sin. We walked the whole road of James 1:13-15, from the source of temptation to the death which sin gives birth to. We did that on purpose. You cannot fight what you cannot see. You cannot prepare for what you do not understand. So we spent nine chapters mapping the road, naming the stops, and watching how each stop turns into the next.

Now the book changes direction. The next four chapters are not about the road downward. They are about the road back up. They are about how to fight at every stop, how to refuse to walk the road one more time, how to walk a different road instead.

Wake Up and Watch

The first thing the watchman does is watch.

Peter put it like this:

> *"Be sober, be vigilant; because your adversary the devil, as a roaring lion, walketh about, seeking whom he may devour."* (1 Peter 5:8)

Two commands in one sentence. *Be sober.* That word, in Greek, means clear-headed, awake, not under the influence of anything that would dull your perception. *Be vigilant.* That word means alert, watchful, on guard. Peter is telling Christians to live as a watchman on a tower. Eyes open. Mind clear. Looking around. Not asleep. Not drunk on anything. Not distracted by anything that would take his attention off the road and the horizon.

Most of us live the opposite of this. We live half asleep. We live with our eyes glued to our screens. We live with our perception dulled by entertainment, by exhaustion, by the slow drip of a culture that wants us anesthetized. We are the watchman on the tower, but we are facing the wrong way, with our eyes closed, with our ears full of music, we have plugged in to keep ourselves from having to hear anything coming.

The lion is real. The lion walks. The lion is looking for someone to devour, and a sleeping watchman is exactly what the lion is hoping to find.

The first move of the cure is to wake up.

Recognize the Pattern

There is a kind of pattern recognition that every Christian has to develop, and the rest of this chapter is about teaching you what it looks like.

You have a road that you walk. The road has the same stops every time. The pull always shows up in the same kinds of moments. The bait always wears the same kinds of dresses. The slow circle always lasts about the same number of laps. The conception always happens in the same kinds of settings. The act always looks the same way. The death always grows in the same way. There is one or two main sins in your life, and each has a road, worn into the ground by you walking it for years.

You can see it if you look.

When did your last fall happen? Walk yourself back through it slowly. Where were you when the pull first showed up? What time of day was it? What kind of mood were you in? Were you tired? Were you hungry? Were you alone? Were you with somebody specific? Was it after a fight? Was it after a victory? Was it after a long stretch of doing well? Was it the day of a deadline? Was it on a weekend, on a weeknight, in the morning, in the late evening? Where was your phone? What had you been watching, listening to, scrolling through, talking about for the hour leading up to it?

Now do the same thing for the fall before that one. And the one before that one. And the one before that one.

If you go through that exercise for fifteen minutes, you will start to see the pattern. The pulls do not happen randomly. The falls do not happen randomly. Some conditions set the table, and the conditions repeat. Maybe yours is always after a Saturday afternoon when nobody is home. Maybe yours is always when a particular friend texts you. Maybe yours is always when you have not slept enough for three days in a row. Maybe yours is always after a fight with your wife or your mom. Maybe yours is always when you have just gotten paid. Maybe yours is always on a long drive. Maybe yours is always at three o'clock in the morning when your phone is on the bedside table, and you cannot sleep.

The pattern is yours. Nobody else has exactly the same one. But the pattern exists, and if you watch yourself with the eyes of a watchman, you can see it.

Watch and Pray

This is what Jesus meant when he told the disciples to watch and pray.

> *"Watch and pray, that ye enter not into temptation: the spirit indeed is willing, but the flesh is weak."* (Matthew 26:41)

He said this in the garden of Gethsemane, on the night that he was betrayed. He had taken Peter, James, and John deeper into the garden than the rest of the disciples, and he had asked them to stay awake and pray with him while he prayed. He came back three different times that night and found them sleeping. Each time he woke them up. Each time, he urged them to watch and pray. Each time, they could not stay awake.

A few hours later, Peter was warming his hands at a fire in the courtyard of the high priest, denying that he had ever known Jesus. Three times. To three different people.

Jesus had warned him this would happen. Jesus had told him at the supper, *"Simon, Simon, behold, Satan hath desired to have you, that he may sift you as wheat: But I have prayed for thee, that thy faith fail not"* (Luke 22:31-32). Jesus had told him in the garden, "Watch and pray." Peter slept. The pattern caught up with him by morning.

Watch and pray are paired in that verse for a reason. Watching alone is not enough. Praying alone is not enough. This is not heresy to say either. The two of them go together. The watchman on the tower has to keep his eyes open AND call down to his Lord. He has to see what is coming, AND ask for the strength to do something about it. Either one without the other will leave him exposed.

You are doing the same thing in this book. Reading is watching. Praying is what turns the watching into something more than just observation. The Lord answers the prayers of the man who is willing to watch. The Lord builds strength into the one who keeps asking.

Let me put this where you live.

Here is something you can do this week, and the week after, and every week for the rest of your life, if you will. Keep a small record of your falls. Just a few sentences. The date. Where were you? What time was it? What had been happening in the hours and days leading up to it? What was the bait dressed as? How many laps did you take? What you told yourself before the act. What you told yourself afterward.

Most Christians never do this. Most Christians want to forget the fall as fast as possible. They confess it to the Lord. They feel the relief of forgiveness. They stand up. They walk away. They do not look back. The next time they fall, they have forgotten the details of the last fall, and they cannot see the pattern that connects them. They are walking the same road. They cannot see that the road repeats.

You will not fight a pattern you have not named.

The record does not have to be long. It does not have to be poetic or beautifully written. It can be a few notes in the back of your Bible, or in a journal nobody else will read, or in a private file on your computer. The point is to gather the data. The point is to start seeing what your road actually looks like. After three or four falls are written down, you will start seeing the pattern. After ten, you will know it. You will know which days are dangerous for you. You will know which moods, settings, times, and baits. You will know yourself the way the watchman on the tower knows the country around his city. You will be able to see things coming before they get close.

That is when the real fight gets easier. Not easy. Easier. Seeing it coming at you as a watchman should be half the battle. You cannot dodge a punch you do not see. You cannot turn off a road you did not know you were on.

Identify the Windows

Here is the second thing you can do, and it is closely related.

Identify your high-risk windows.

Every Christian has windows of time when they are more vulnerable than others. The data from your fall log will tell you what yours are. For most young people, the high-risk windows are predictable. Late nights when nobody is up. Weekends with no schedule. Days right after an emotional blow, like a fight, a disappointment, or a rejection. The first hour of being alone after a long day around people. Long drives. Hotel rooms. Vacations. Times when your normal accountability is not in place, when nobody is watching, when nobody knows where you are or what you are doing.

These windows are not sinful in and of themselves. There is nothing wrong with being alone. There is nothing wrong with a Saturday afternoon. There is nothing wrong with a hotel room, a long drive, or a vacation. But these windows are when your particular fall is most likely to happen, and the watchman on the tower needs to be especially awake during these windows of time.

When you can see one of those windows coming, plan ahead. Decide before the window opens what you will do during it. Plan to be around people. Plan to leave the phone in another room. Plan to text someone you trust at a certain time. Plan to get out of the house. Plan to read a chapter of the Bible. Plan something. The unplanned high-risk window is where the lust does its best work. The planned high-risk window is one the lust has to fight uphill against your own preparation.

Pre-deciding how you will act before it attacks is the most important thing you can do here.

We will spend more time on this in the next chapter, when we talk about Daniel and pre-decision. For now, just notice the windows. Just start watching for them. Just start seeing them as windows.

Seeing What You Can't See

Here is the third thing that you need to do. Get help seeing what you cannot see.

The watchman on the tower had a partner most of the time. He had other men on the walls. He had a relief shift scheduled when his hours ended. He had a network of watchers in other towns who could send signals to him by fire at night, the way you read about in the book of Judges. No watchman in ancient Israel was alone. The whole point of the watchman system was that everybody was watching together.

You cannot see your own pattern as someone who loves you can. You have blind spots. You are inside your own life. You cannot watch yourself sleeping. You cannot watch yourself when your phone is in your hand at midnight. You cannot watch yourself through the eyes of someone who knows you well and has known you for years.

This is why the Hebrew writer says, *"But exhort one another daily, while it is called To day; lest any of you be hardened through the deceitfulness of sin"* (Hebrews 3:13). Sin is deceitful. It deceives the man who carries it, often more than it deceives anybody else. The man who is being hardened by sin is usually the last to see it. He needs another Christian who is willing to tell him hard things. He needs an elder who will ask hard questions. He needs a friend who will say, *"I have noticed something in you the last few months, and I want to talk to you about it."*

Find that person. Find that group. Get into a relationship with one or two faithful Christians who know you well enough to see what you cannot see, and humble enough to tell you the truth, and trustworthy enough that what you say to them will not get back to anyone else. This is one of the great gifts of the local church. The body has eyes. Use the eyes the body has.

If you do not have anybody like that right now, start praying for one. Tell the Lord you need help seeing yourself, and you cannot do it alone, and you need a brother or a sister who can be a watchman with you on the wall. The Lord answers prayers like that. He has been answering them since Genesis. He gave Adam Eve. He gave David Jonathan. He gave Paul Timothy. He gave Naomi Ruth. He will give you somebody. Ask.

Before you turn the page toward the next chapter, do one thing. Go back through your last fall in your mind. Walk through it slowly. See if you can find the pattern in it. See if you can see, in hindsight, the moments where you should have seen it coming. That is the eyes of a watchman. That is the first thing a watchman has to learn. You can see it now. The next one, you can see while it is still on the horizon.

The June bug never had this option. The June bug had no watchman on his tower. He had no eyes for the pattern. He had no Bible to teach him what the light of the bug zapper was actually doing to him. You have all of those. Use them.

The road has been mapped. The watchtower has been built. The watchman has been called.

Wake up.

For Discussion

1. Read Ezekiel 33:7. What does it mean to be a watchman over your own soul? How does that picture change the way you think about temptation?

2. Read 1 Peter 5:8. What does it mean to be sober and vigilant in a culture that does everything possible to dull your perception? What in your daily life makes the watchman role harder for you?

3. Walk yourself slowly through your last fall. What were the conditions leading up to it? What time of day, what mood, what setting? What pattern do you see when you do this?

4. The chapter recommends keeping a small fall log. What is your honest reaction to that idea? What would it cost you to start one this week?

5. What are your high-risk windows? Be specific. Days, times, settings, moods. Once you have named them, what is one practical thing you can do to prepare for the next one?

6. Read Hebrews 3:13. Who in your life is positioned to see what you cannot see in yourself? If nobody is, what is your next step in finding that person?

Chapter 11

Decide Before You Have To

Daniel was most likely around fourteen years old when his city fell.

He was a noble boy from the tribe of Judah, raised in Jerusalem, taught the law from his earliest memories. He had grown up watching the priests in the temple, hearing the songs of David in the house of the Lord, eating only the food the law of Moses said an Israelite was permitted to eat. The boundaries of his life had been clear from the time he could walk. There was clean and unclean. There was permitted and forbidden. There was the way of the Lord, and there was every other way.

Then the army of Babylon broke down the walls of Jerusalem.

Nebuchadnezzar marched into the city. He took the gold of the temple. He took the books of the prophets. He took the strongest, brightest, most promising young men he could find among the captives, and he took them back to Babylon to be trained for the king's service. Daniel was one of them. So was his friend Hananiah, who would later be called Shadrach. So was Mishael, who would later be called Meshach. So was Azariah, who would later be called Abed-nego. They were marched a thousand miles east, along the same road the rest of Israel would walk in the years that followed, and they were brought into a palace where everything they had ever known was gone.

The king assigned them new names. The king assigned them new tutors. The king assigned them three years of training in the language and learning of the Chaldeans. He fed them at his own table. He gave them the wine of his own house and the meat from his own kitchens. They were being groomed for the highest service in his kingdom.

Then Daniel did one of the most quietly heroic things in the entire Old Testament.

> *"But Daniel purposed in his heart that he would not defile himself with the portion of the king's meat, nor with the wine which he drank: therefore he requested of the prince of the eunuchs that he might not defile himself."* (Daniel 1:8)

Daniel purposed in his heart.

That phrase is what this whole chapter is about.

Daniel did not stand there at the king's table on the first night, trying to figure out what to do.

He did not look at the wine and weigh whether the law really meant what it said when it was written for an Israelite who had a temple in Jerusalem and a country of his own. He did not look at the meat and try to remember whether his rabbi had ever taught him about exceptions in foreign palaces. He did not stand there, with three thousand years of Jewish history pressing on his shoulders, and decide in the heat of the moment what he would do.

The decision had already been made in his mind. Long before the meat and wine ever hit the table, Daniel had decided. *Purposed in his heart* is the behavior of a man who had a settled answer waiting before the question ever arrived. By the time the king's food was put in front of him, all Daniel had to do was speak the answer he had already chosen.

That is the whole secret of this chapter. That is the whole strategy of fighting at this stop on the road.

You decide before you have to.

Most Christians lose the battle with sin and temptation because they try to make the decision in the moment.

The bait is in front of them. The pull is on them. The slow circle has started. Now, in the worst possible conditions for clear thinking, with the lust awake and the dress on the bait and the body already responding, they try to decide what to do. They try to weigh the decision in front of them. They try to reason. They try to figure out what the Lord would want from them in this specific situation.

It is the worst time in the world to make any decision.

A man does not buy a fire extinguisher while his house is on fire. A football team does not write its playbook in the middle of the fourth quarter. A pilot does not study the emergency procedures while the plane is going down. The time to make hard decisions is not when the pressure is at its highest. The time to make hard decisions is in advance, when your head is clear, when the bait is not in front of you, when the lust is not awake, when you can think the way a Christian is supposed to be able to think.

Daniel did this. Joseph did this. Job did this when he made *"a covenant with mine eyes; why then should I think upon a maid?"* (Job 31:1). David did this in his good seasons. Paul did this when he wrote, *"But I keep under my body, and bring it into subjection: lest that by any means, when I have preached to others, I myself should be a castaway"* (1 Corinthians 9:27). The men in the Bible who walked well, walked well because they had decided to walk well long before the moments that tested them.

The men who walked badly were those still deciding when the moment came.

Esau was the opposite of Daniel.

Esau was the older brother of Jacob, the firstborn son of Isaac, the man who carried the birthright of the covenant family. He was a hunter and a man of the field. He was strong, rough, and good at what he did. The text says his father loved him because his father loved venison.

One day, Esau came in from the field, tired and hungry. Jacob was at home cooking a stew of red lentils. The smell hit Esau as he walked through the door. He had been gone all day with no food, and the smell of that stew was the closest thing to a feast he had encountered in hours.

He asked Jacob for some.

Jacob, sharper and more calculating than his older brother, saw an opportunity. He said he would trade. He would give Esau the stew in exchange for the birthright. The birthright was the greater inheritance, the spiritual leadership of the family, the line through which the promises of God to Abraham would flow. It was worth more than anything any son in the ancient Near East could possess.

Esau looked at the stew. He looked at his hunger. He made the trade in the moment.

> *"And Esau said, Behold, I am at the point to die: and what profit shall this birthright do to me? And Jacob said, Swear to me this day; and he sware unto him: and he sold his birthright unto Jacob. Then Jacob gave Esau bread and pottage of lentiles; and he did eat and drink, and rose up, and went his way: thus Esau despised his birthright."* (Genesis 25:32-34)

The Hebrew writer comments on this fourteen hundred years later, and the comment cuts:

> *"Lest there be any fornicator, or profane person, as Esau, who for one morsel of meat sold his birthright. For ye know how that afterward, when he would have inherited the blessing, he was rejected: for he found no place of repentance, though he sought it carefully with tears."* (Hebrews 12:16-17)

Esau did not lose the birthright because he was unintelligent. He lost it because he decided in the moment. He had not purposed in his heart anything about the birthright. He had not thought it through in advance. He had not settled the question, *if I am ever offered something for my birthright, what is my answer?* He came home hungry and tired, and the smell of stew was in the air, and the question was put to him, and he had to decide right then. The conditions were terrible. He did what most men do under terrible conditions when making decisions. He chose the immediate over the eternal.

The contrast with Daniel could not be sharper. Daniel was offered the king's meat at fourteen years old in a foreign palace where his life was at the mercy of his captors. He had every reason to capitulate. He chose otherwise. He chose otherwise because he had already chosen otherwise long before the meat ever showed up.

You will be Daniel, or you will be Esau, in your own ways, a thousand times in your life. The difference between them is the difference between purposing in your heart in advance and purposing in your heart in the moment. One method works. The other one rarely does.

Joshua, at the very end of his life, gathered all of Israel together at Shechem and called them to the same kind of pre-decision.

> *"And if it seem evil unto you to serve the Lord, choose you this day whom ye will serve; whether the gods which your fathers served that were on the other side of the flood, or the gods of the Amorites, in whose land ye dwell: but as for me and my house, we will serve the Lord."* (Joshua 24:15)

Notice what Joshua does not do. He does not say, *try to do better next time.* He does not say, *be a little stronger when the temptation comes.* He says, *choose this day.* Today. Right now. Decide while you can think clearly. Make it as a household. Make it as a man and his family before the Lord. Make it before the next idol shows up, before the next neighbor invites you to bow down to a foreign god, before the next compromise is offered to you.

A choice you make today does not get tested today. It gets tested tomorrow, next week, and ten years from now, when the situation arises for which the choice was made. A choice you do not make today gets tested the same way, except you will be deciding under fire, in conditions of maximum pressure, with no preparation. The choice still happens either way. The difference is whether the choice gets made in the calm of a Sunday afternoon or in the heat of a Friday night.

Joshua chose for his house. The men of Israel that day chose with him. *And the people said unto Joshua, The Lord our God will we serve, and his voice will we obey* (Joshua 24:24). Many of them broke that promise in the years that followed. Many of them kept it. The point is that they had something to break or keep. They had a settled answer. They had stuck a flag in the ground. The next generation that came along after Joshua died, the text says in Judges, was a generation that *"knew not the Lord, nor yet the works which he had done for Israel"* (Judges 2:10). They had no purposed answer. They had nothing pre-decided. They walked the road of the nations around them, because they had not chosen any other road.

Application

You can do what Daniel did. You can do it in the next ten minutes if you are willing.

Take a piece of paper, or open a new note on your phone, and write at the top of it the words *I have purposed in my heart.* Then list, slowly, prayerfully, the decisions you are making in advance. Make the list specific. Make the list honest. Make the list strong enough that when the moment comes, the decision is already made, and all you have to do is execute it.

Some examples of what your list might look like:

I have purposed in my heart that I will not look at pornography. Not late at night, not when I am tired, not when I am stressed, not when I am alone in a hotel room, not ever. The decision is made.

I have purposed in my heart that I will not be alone in a room with a girl who is not my wife. Not for any reason. Not for any length of time. Not even if it would be embarrassing to leave the room, the decision is made.

I have purposed in my heart that I will not drink with my coworkers at the company event next week. I will order a coffee or a soda. I will not explain myself unless somebody asks. The decision is made.

I have purposed in my heart that I will not raise my voice to my wife or my children when I am angry. Not because they always deserve calm, but because losing my temper is not who I am going to be. The decision is made.

I have purposed in my heart that I will read a chapter of the Bible every morning before I look at my phone. The decision is made.

You will notice something about those statements. They are not vague. They are not aspirational. They are not *I will try to,* or *I am going to work on it.* They are decisions, made in advance, with the same kind of grammar Daniel used. *Purposed in heart* is not a wish. It is a verdict.

The verdict goes into the ground like a stake. It does not move when the bait shows up. It does not move when lust awakens. It does not move when the slow circle starts. The decision was made before the bait, before the lust, before the circle. The verdict is what you walked into the day with. The verdict is what the moment cannot change, because the moment was not where the decision was made.

Here is the second thing about pre-decision. It works because it is paired with Scripture.

David said it like this:

> *"Thy word have I hid in mine heart, that I might not sin against thee."* (Psalm 119:11)

A purposed decision in your heart is much stronger when it is built on a verse of Scripture in your heart. The decision is yours, but the foundation is the Lord's. The decision is your *yes* and your *no*. The foundation is *Thus saith the Lord*. The two of them go together, the way watching and praying go together. One alone is not enough. The two of them together are how a Christian holds his ground.

So pair every decision with a verse.

I have purposed in my heart not to look at pornography, because Job said, "I made a covenant with mine eyes; why then should I think upon a maid?" (Job 31:1).

I have purposed in my heart not to drink at company events, because Solomon said, "Wine is a mocker, strong drink is raging: and whosoever is deceived thereby is not wise" (Proverbs 20:1).

I have purposed in my heart not to raise my voice at my family, because Paul said, "Let all bitterness, and wrath, and anger, and clamour, and evil speaking, be put away from you, with all malice" (Ephesians 4:31).

Memorize the verses. Keep them where you can find them. When the moment comes, you will find that the verse rises up to meet the decision, and the decision is much harder to break than it would have been alone. Jesus showed this in the wilderness. Three baits. Three Words of Scripture. Three escapes. The pre-decision was alive in him because it was paired with the Word.

Here is the third thing about pre-decision. Tell somebody.

A decision spoken out loud to another Christian becomes a stake in the ground, with someone else holding the other end. This is part of why the New Testament is so insistent on Christians having other Christians in their lives. The body holds you accountable. The body remembers what you said. The body asks how you are doing with the things you decided.

If you decided this morning that you would not be alone in a room with someone who is not your wife, tell your wife about the decision. Tell a brother in Christ. Tell one of your elders. The decision in your private journal can be reversed in your private journal. The decision spoken to another believer is much harder to walk back. The other believer becomes a watchman with you on the tower. They cannot do the watching for you, but they can keep you honest about whether you are still on the wall.

Daniel did this. He did not just decide privately. He went to the prince of the eunuchs and told the man what he was going to do (Daniel 1:8). The decision became visible. The decision became something Daniel had to live up to in front of another human being. That is part of what made the decision hold.

The next chapter is about running. Sometimes the pre-decision works. Sometimes you can stand in the moment and execute what you decided in advance. Sometimes the bait is too strong, the lust is too loud, the room is too dangerous, and the only right response is to leave the way Joseph left, with your coat in her hand and your feet pounding out the back door. We will look at how, when, and why to run.

Before you turn the page, write your list. Even a short one. Even three or four lines. Start somewhere. Start tonight.

The June bug never had a list. The June bug had no purpose in his heart. He walked into every summer night with no flag in the ground, no decision made in advance, no Word hid in the heart, no brother in Christ to tell. He flew to the light because nothing in him had been settled. The light was what was in front of him, and what is in front of you is what you will reach for, unless something deeper has already been decided.

You can decide. The Lord is asking you to. *Choose you this day.*

For Discussion

1. Read Daniel 1:8 once more. Notice the order of events: Daniel purposed first, then he requested. Why does the decision have to come before the request? What happens to your strength when the order is reversed?

2. Read Genesis 25:29-34 and Hebrews 12:16-17. Why was Esau's decision in the moment so disastrous? What had he failed to do beforehand?

3. The chapter says you will be Daniel or you will be Esau a thousand times in your life. Where in your life have you been like Daniel? Where have you been like Esau? What was the difference in preparation?

4. Take ten minutes and write your own short *I have purposed in my heart* list. What three or four decisions can you make right now, before the moment comes?

5. Read Psalm 119:11. Pair each of your decisions with a verse of Scripture. Why is the decision stronger when it is paired with the Word?

6. Whom in your life can you tell about the decisions you have made? Why does telling another believer make the decision more durable?

Chapter 12

Run, Don't Negotiate

Joseph was likely about twenty-eight years old when his master's wife grabbed him by the coat.

He had been in Egypt for over a decade by then. He had been sold into slavery as a teenager by his own brothers, hauled across the desert in a caravan of Ishmaelite traders, and bought at auction in the slave market of a wealthy Egyptian official named Potiphar. The text says Potiphar was the captain of the guard for Pharaoh, which means he was a high-ranking military man with a large household, a large estate, and a wife who lived in considerable comfort.

Joseph climbed the ladder fast. The Lord was with him, and Potiphar saw it. By the time the events of Genesis 39 begin, Joseph is the overseer of the entire estate. Potiphar has put everything he owns into Joseph's hands, except the food on his own table, and even that the text mentions almost as an afterthought. Joseph is running the household. Joseph is managing the staff. Joseph is going through every room of the palace every day, doing his master's business.

Then Potiphar's wife noticed him.

The text says Joseph was *"a goodly person, and well favoured"* (Genesis 39:6). He was a handsome man. She saw him every day, walking through her house, doing her husband's business, having full access to every room and every hour of the day. And eventually she did what she had probably been thinking about doing for a long time. She made her move.

> *"And it came to pass after these things, that his master's wife cast her eyes upon Joseph; and she said, Lie with me."* (Genesis 39:7)

Lie with me. That was the bait. That was the dress on the bait, with the hook hidden underneath, and that was the question Joseph had to answer.

Joseph said *no.*

He said *no* with reasons. He said his master had trusted him with everything in the house, and that the only thing his master had kept back from him was the woman herself. He said the act would be a great wickedness and a sin against God. He gave her the answer of a man who had thought about this kind of question long before this kind of question had ever been asked.

Unfortunately, she did not stop. She was relentless.

The text says she pressured him *"day by day"* (Genesis 39:10), the same kind of *daily* pressure Delilah used on Samson. The same kind of relentless, repetitive, wearing-down kind of pressure that the slow circle is made of. This was the classic Steve Urkel move. She did not just ask him once. She asked him every day. She positioned herself near him. She found reasons to be in the same rooms as he was. She made the bait constant.

Joseph did one thing that Samson did not do. He refused to stay near her.

> *"And it came to pass, as she spake to Joseph day by day, that he hearkened not unto her, to lie by her, or to be with her.* (Genesis 39:10)

Joseph would not lie with her, but he also would not even be with her. He did not stay in the room. He did not test the trap. He did not see how strong he was tonight. He created distance. He kept his shifts in the parts of the house she was not in. He did his work and got out. He did not give the slow circle anywhere to start.

Then came the day she caught him alone.

> *"And it came to pass about this time, that Joseph went into the house to do his business; and there was none of the men of the house there within. And she caught him by his garment, saying, Lie with me: and he left his garment in her hand, and fled, and got him out."* (Genesis 39:11-12)

Joseph did not negotiate.

He did not try to talk her into letting go. He did not stop to put together a careful argument. He did not weigh whether running might cause some administrative problem in the household. He did not stand there reasoning with her about why this was a bad idea. He left his coat in her hand and ran. The coat was a small price to pay for his integrity, his life, and his standing before God.

She was holding his coat when he hit the door.

That is the picture for this chapter.

The Bible tells Christians to flee from sin. It does not tell them to fight every fight. It does not tell them to test their strength. It does not tell them to see how close they can get without falling. There is a category of sin where the right response is to put your head down and run, and the New Testament names it more than once.

"Flee also youthful lusts: but follow righteousness, faith, charity, peace, with them that call on the Lord out of a pure heart." (2 Timothy 2:22)

"Flee fornication. Every sin that a man doeth is without the body; but he that committeth fornication sinneth against his own body." (1 Corinthians 6:18)

"Wherefore, my dearly beloved, flee from idolatry." (1 Corinthians 10:14)

Three different times and three different categories. Sexual sin, idolatry, the lusts of youth. The Greek verb for 'flee' is *pheugō*. It means to run, to escape, to take flight. It is the same verb a person would use about running from a fire, or running from a wild animal, or running from an army. It is not a strategic, dignified withdrawal. It is a flat-out run.

That is how the Bible tells you to handle certain kinds of temptation.

Most Christians do not want to hear this because they have been raised on a kind of Christian masculinity that prizes standing your ground. They have been taught that fleeing is for cowards, that real men hold their position, that backing down from a fight is a kind of failure. They are willing to be told to fight harder. They are not so willing to be told to run faster.

The Bible does not share this view. The Bible says you fight some battles and you flee others. There are sins where the right thing to do is dig in. There are sins for which the right thing to do is to leave the building. The wisdom of the Christian life is knowing which is which.

Sexual sin, the New Testament says repeatedly, is the kind you flee. Lust of all sorts is the kind you flee. The fight at this stop on the road is not the fight to stay in the room. The fight at this stop on the road is the fight to get out.

Why is fleeing the right response to certain sins?

It is because of what we said in the chapter on the slow circle. The longer you stay near the bait, the harder it gets to leave. The lust feeds on proximity. The lust quiets when there is distance and grows louder when there is closeness. The conception we talked about in chapter seven happens to a heart that has lingered. It does not usually happen to a heart that has been a hundred yards away from the bait the whole time.

Joseph understood this. He did not stay in the room with Potiphar's wife to test his resolve. He kept his distance for as long as he could. When the day finally came that distance was no longer possible, when she had cornered him in an empty house with her hand on his coat, he understood that the time for keeping distance was over and the time for running was now. He left the coat, he hit the door, and he got out.

Samson clearly did not understand this. He kept coming back to Delilah. He kept testing the trap. He kept seeing how close he could get without losing what he had. He thought he could manage the proximity.

The line between Joseph and Samson is the line between a man who flees and a man who lingers. That line has run through every Christian life since the New Testament was written.

Application

You have to know what fleeing looks like for your particular fight. Fleeing is not a single behavior. Fleeing is whatever it takes to get distance between you and the bait that has been working on you. The shape of the running depends on the shape of the lust.

If your fight is with pornography, fleeing might look like installing accountability software on every device you own, including the ones you have hidden from yourself. It might look like throwing your private device in the river. It might look like canceling subscriptions. It might look like never being on a phone, a tablet, or a laptop after a certain hour at night. It might look like making sure you are never alone with a screen in your hand in a private room with the door closed. It might look like getting up and walking outside when the urge hits, even if you are wearing slippers and it is raining.

If your fight is with alcohol, fleeing should look like never having any in your house, never going to social events where you know it will be present, and never being alone with a friend who drinks. It might look like asking for a different table at a restaurant, or leaving a wedding reception early, or saying no to an invitation you have said yes to in the past.

If your fight is with a particular relationship that should not exist, the kind that everybody around you has been quietly worried about, fleeing might look like cutting all contact. Not less contact. All contact. No texting. No following on social media. No accidental running into. No staying friends. No holding on for the sake of old times ' sake. Joseph did not stay friends with Potiphar's wife. He left his coat behind, and he did not go back for it.

If your fight is with anger, fleeing might look like leaving the room when you feel the heat rising, before you say something you cannot take back. It might look like getting in the car and driving for ten minutes. It might look like telling your wife, *I need to step out for a minute*, and walking outside until your hands stop shaking.

The shape of the fleeing fits the shape of the lust. The point is not the specific tactic. The point is that fleeing is real, fleeing is biblical, and fleeing is sometimes and oftentimes the only thing that works.

Some people will tell you that fleeing is a sign of weakness. They will say a strong Christian does not run, that a strong Christian stands his ground, that fleeing is what Christians did in the old days when they had real faith. They will say you need to learn to handle these things head-on.

They are wrong.

The Bible says flee. The Bible does not apologize for saying flee. The Bible says flee three different times in different letters from different writers in different cities, all of which had Christians who needed to hear it. The wisest, godliest men in the New Testament knew that running was sometimes the right move.

Paul fled from Damascus through a window down the wall in a basket when the Jews were trying to kill him there (Acts 9:25). Paul fled from Lystra after he was stoned and left for dead (Acts 14:20). Paul fled from Thessalonica when the mob came after him (Acts 17:10). The apostle who wrote *flee fornication* knew what fleeing looked like in his own life. He was not ashamed to do it when the moment called for it.

Jesus himself fled. As a baby, his parents fled with him into Egypt to escape Herod's slaughter of the innocents (Matthew 2:13-14). As an adult, he withdrew from cities that were planning his death because his hour had not yet come (John 7:1, John 10:39). He stood his ground when the time came to stand. He withdrew when the time came to withdraw. The wisdom was knowing the difference.

If Jesus fled, you can flee. If Paul fled, you can flee. The Christian who refuses to flee because he thinks fleeing is beneath him is the Christian who is going to lose, because he has substituted his own pride for the Bible's strategy.

There is one more thing to say about fleeing.

When you flee, you do not flee to nothing. You flee ***to*** something. Look at the verse from 2 Timothy again:

> *"Flee also youthful lusts: but follow righteousness, faith, charity, peace, with them that call on the Lord out of a pure heart."* (2 Timothy 2:22)

Notice the structure. Flee from this. Follow that. Run from one place. Run to another. Paul does not just say *get away*. He says *get away to something*. Run from the lust and run to righteousness. Run from the bait. Run to faith and love and peace. Run from the lonely room. Run to the company of believers who are seeking the Lord with you.

Most people who try to flee without a destination end up flowing right back into the place they were trying to leave. A vacuum gets filled. If you take pornography out of your life and put nothing in its place, the lust will find something else to land on, because the lust has not gone away. If you cut the wrong relationship out of your life and do not put a healthy relationship in its place, the lonely place inside you that the wrong relationship was filling will find some other wrong thing to fill it.

So when you flee, decide where you are running to. Run to the Word. Run to the assembly. Run to a brother in Christ who will pray with you. Run to the work of your hands, the labor that takes your mind off the lust and puts it on something useful. Run to the people of God. The whole point of the church is that there is somewhere to run to. The body of Christ is a place where the man who has fled from lust can land and breathe.

We will spend more time on this in the next and final chapter. The brighter light is what you run to. The bug zapper is what you run from. The whole point of the Christian life, in one sense, is that we have somewhere brighter to be than the porch near the bug zapper!

Joseph fled, and he ended up in prison.

Potiphar's wife was furious that he had run. She kept the coat. She showed it to her servants and to her husband and accused Joseph of attacking her. Potiphar believed her, or at least pretended to, and threw Joseph in the king's prison. Joseph spent two more years in chains for a sin he had refused to commit.

But the same chapter that ends with him in prison also says, *"the Lord was with Joseph, and shewed him mercy, and gave him favour in the sight of the keeper of the prison"* (Genesis 39:21). And from that prison, Joseph eventually walked into the throne room of Pharaoh. From that throne room, he eventually saved the entire ancient world from a famine. From that famine, he eventually rescued his own family. This family had sold him into slavery, the family God had promised would become a nation that would bring forth the Messiah of the world.

That whole story rests on a coat in a woman's hand and a young man running for the door.

You will not always see the rest of the story right away. Joseph did not. He sat in that prison for a long time, probably wondering whether his integrity had been worth what it had cost him. Sometimes you flee, and you end up in a prison that does not feel any better than the room you fled. Sometimes you flee, and the people around you misunderstand what you did. Sometimes you flee, and the cost of fleeing seems higher in the short term than the cost of staying would have been.

The Lord sees, and the Lord remembers. The Lord turns the running away from sin into a story that does not always make sense in the moment but does in the long view. "

And we know that all things work together for good to them that love God, to them that are the called according to his purpose" (Romans 8:28). Including the running—especially the running, when the running was for him.

The June bug never had a door to run for. The June bug had nowhere else to be. The porch zapper was the only light in his world.

You have a door. You have somewhere to run to. The Lord has set the door open. The Word has told you to flee. Run towards the brighter light than the bug zapper. The body of Christ is waiting on the other side.

Run.

Discussion Questions

1. Read Genesis 39:7-12. What did Joseph do *before* the day of the seizure that prepared him to run when the moment came? How does pre-decision (chapter eleven) connect to fleeing (chapter twelve)?

2. The Bible says *flee* in 2 Timothy 2:22, 1 Corinthians 6:18, and 1 Corinthians 10:14. Why does the New Testament use that word? Why not *resist* or *stand firm*?

3. Compare Samson and Joseph one more time. Both faced daily pressure. One stayed. One fled. Why is the difference between them the most important difference in this whole book?

4. The chapter says fleeing is not weakness. Have you ever thought of running as something a strong Christian shouldn't have to do? Where did that idea come from?

5. What does fleeing look like, specifically, for your particular fight? Be concrete. What would you have to walk away from this week, and how would you do it?

6. Read 2 Timothy 2:22 again. What are you fleeing *to*? What does that landing place look like in your life right now? If you do not have one, what is your next step in finding one?

Chapter 13

A Brighter Light

Go back to the porch scene with the bug zapper and the June bug one more time.

The blue bug zapper is still humming under the eaves. The boards of the porch are still warped. The bugs are still finding the light, the way they always do. But this time, look up.

The moon is out tonight. It is high, round, and white against a clear summer sky. It is the only natural light source for a hundred miles in any direction, and it is enormous, and it has been there every night since the fourth day of creation. The world is full of moonlight. Trees are silvered with it. The barn roof is silvered with it. The pond at the edge of the property is throwing a long, slow column of moonlight back up at the sky like a mirror set on the ground.

The June bug never sees any of this.

The June bug only sees the zapper. The zapper is closer. The zapper is brighter, in the immediate sense of being a few feet from him instead of a few hundred thousand miles. The zapper hums, the hum gets in his head, the orbiting begins, and by the time he hits the wires, he never even notices the big, bright moon giving off pure light.

That has been the picture of the whole book. The bug zapper is sin. The pull of the zapper is the pull of the lust meeting the bait. The slow circle is the lap before the lap. The contact is the act. The pile of bodies on the boards by morning is the death sin gives birth to. We have walked the road, named the stops, learned how to fight at every one. We are at the end of the road now.

But the June bug never knew there was anything else.

But God be thanked, you now do.

Paul wrote it like this:

> *"For God, who commanded the light to shine out of darkness, hath shined in our hearts, to give the light of the knowledge of the glory of God in the face of Jesus Christ."* (2 Corinthians 4:6)

The same God who said *let there be light* on the first day of creation has spoken light into the heart of every Christian. The light is the knowledge of his glory. The face of Christ is where the light comes through. We are not out on a porch with no other option. We are standing under a moon the size of the cosmos, and the light on us has been shining since before the foundation of the world.

The whole reason the bug zapper has so much pull on most Christians is that they are not actually living in the light. They know about the light. They have heard about the light. They have sung songs about the light their whole lives. But they have not put themselves in a position where the light is what they live in, day in and day out, hour by hour, conversation by conversation, decision by decision.

The bug zapper has the easiest time pulling a Christian who has never really moved his porch swing into the moonlight.

You cannot win the fight against sin by fighting against sin alone.

That has been the implicit message of the whole second half of this book, and we are going to make it explicit now. Watching is good. Pre-deciding is vital. Running is essential. All of those are real strategies, and the Bible commands every one of them. But none of them, by themselves, kills the lust. None of them, by themselves, breaks the deeper hunger that has been driving the lust the whole time. None of them, by themselves, gives you a new heart to live out of.

Watching keeps the lust from surprising you. Pre-deciding keeps you from being unarmed when it comes. Running keeps you from staying near it long enough to fall. Those are real victories. But the lust is still alive in you while you are doing all of those things. You are managing a beast that is still in the cage with you.

The only way to kill the beast is to feed something else.

> *"And be not conformed to this world: but be ye transformed by the renewing of your mind, that ye may prove what is that good, and acceptable, and perfect, will of God."* (Romans 12:2)

Paul does not say *try harder.* He does not say *resist more.* He says *be transformed by the renewing of your mind.* The transformation comes from the renewing. The renewing is what the Word of God does to a Christian who reads it, prays about it, sings it, hears it preached, talks about it with other believers, and lives in it the way a fish lives in water.

A renewed mind starts to want different things. A renewed mind starts to be moved by different things. A renewed mind starts to find the bug zapper less interesting and the moon more beautiful, not because anybody told it to, but because the Word has begun to reshape what the mind is even capable of finding attractive. The fight against sin becomes easier because the very desires that once drove it are beginning to die at the root.

The Lord is not just trying to get you to behave better. He is trying to remake you. He is shining light into hearts that have been in darkness, and the light, given time and opportunity, is going to make those hearts unable to live in the dark the way they used to.

The Word of God is the central instrument in this work.

Read Psalm 119, the longest chapter in the Bible. The whole psalm is about one thing. It is about what the Word does in a man who lives in it and by it. The psalmist talks about the Word of God as a lamp to his feet and a light to his path (Psalm 119:105). He talks about the Word being sweeter than honey to his mouth (Psalm 119:103). He talks about hiding the Word in his heart so he might not sin against God (Psalm 119:11). He says, *"How shall a young man cleanse his way? by taking heed thereto according to thy word"* (Psalm 119:9).

That last verse is the key verse for this whole book.

A young man cleanses his way by the Word. Not by trying harder. Not by being more sincere. Not by feeling more guilty. By the Word. The Word is the cleansing agent. The Word is what the Spirit of God uses to scrub the lust out of the heart over time. The Word is what fills the cisterns that the bait keeps trying to drain.

If you do not read your Bible, you will not have a renewed mind. There is no shortcut to this. There is no spiritual experience, no church program, no accountability software, no friend, no preacher, no mentor that can substitute for the Word being in your life. The Word has to be in you, every day, for years, for the renewing to do its work.

If you have not been doing this, start right now, in this very moment. Pick a chapter of the Bible. Read it. Pray about it. Read another tomorrow. Do not measure yourself against any goal except this question: Did *I read it today?* The renewal happens slowly. The renewing happens by the process of accumulation. The renewing happens to the man who shows up to the page over and over again, and lets the Word do what only the Word can do.

The second instrument is the assembly of God's people.

> *"And let us consider one another to provoke unto love and to good works: not forsaking the assembling of ourselves together, as the manner of some is; but exhorting one another: and so much the more, as ye see the day approaching."* (Hebrews 10:24-25)

You cannot do this alone.

The whole New Testament assumes that the Christian life is a life lived in the body. The local church is not optional. The local church is not a social activity for people who happen to like religion. The local church is the family of God, the bride of Christ, the household of faith, the community where the love of Christ becomes visible in the love of brothers and sisters for each other. It is the place where the renewing of the mind gets reinforced by the Word being preached, the songs being sung, the table of the Lord being shared, and the prayers of the saints being lifted up together.

The June bug had no swarm. The June bug flew alone. He died alone, and there was no other June bug to mourn him or warn the next one not to do the same thing.

You have a swarm. You have a body. You have people. The Lord has saved you into a community. The community is where you watch with other watchmen, where you decide together what no household among you will serve, where you find the brothers and sisters who will help you flee from what you have to flee from. The Christian who tries to fight the lust in isolation has cut himself off from one of the main weapons God gave him.

Be at services. Be there when the doors are open. Be involved in the work. Find a class to attend. Find a group to study with. Find people you can call when you are tempted at midnight. Find an elder who will know your name and ask you how you are doing in the things that actually matter. The renewing of the mind happens in the community of God's people. The light is brighter when many lights are gathered.

The third instrument is the active replacement of what the lust used to feed on.

> *"Finally, brethren, whatsoever things are true, whatsoever things are honest, whatsoever things are just, whatsoever things are pure, whatsoever things are lovely, whatsoever things are of good report; if*

> *there be any virtue, and if there be any praise, think on these things."* (Philippians 4:8)

Paul gives Christians a list of categories that the renewed mind is supposed to fill itself with. *True. Honest. Just. Pure. Lovely. Of good report.* Six categories. The point of the list is not the categories themselves. The point is that the mind will think about something, and Paul wants Christians to be intentional about what they fill it with.

The lust eats whatever you feed it. If you feed it the things on Paul's list, it gets weaker. If you feed it the things from the bait, it gets stronger. There is no neutral. There is no in-between space where you can let the mind drift and expect the lust to leave you alone.

So fill your hours with things that point to God. Fill your eyes with clean things. Fill your ears with wholesome things. Fill your conversations with things that build up rather than tear down. Fill your hands with work that matters. Fill your home with people who love the Lord. Fill your evenings with the Bible and your mornings with prayer. Fill the spaces in your week that the bait used to live in with something the bait cannot survive in.

The lust dies when it is starved. The lust grows when it is fed. The renewing of the mind is, in one sense, just the disciplined practice of feeding the right things and starving the wrong ones, day after day, week after week, year after year, until the lust is a smaller voice than it used to be.

If you are not yet a Christian, this last chapter has to take a turn.

Everything we have said in the second half of this book assumes that the person reading has been brought into Christ. The watchman on the tower, the pre-decision in the heart, the running for the door, the renewing of the mind, the assembly of the saints, the active replacement of the bait with the Word, all of those depend on a man being in Christ first. Without that, the strategies do not have the power they were designed to have. They are the right strategies, but they are run on the wrong fuel.

If you have read this whole book and you have never come to the Lord on the Lord's terms, the road of sin is still complete in your life from start to finish. The death is not theoretical for you. The wages have been paid, but the blood from the cross has not been applied. The whole gospel of Jesus Christ is held out to you right now, the way it has been held out to every sinner since the day of Pentecost.

> *"Then Peter said unto them, Repent, and be baptized every one of you in the name of Jesus Christ for the remission of sins, and ye shall receive the gift of the Holy Ghost."* (Acts 2:38)

The book of Acts is full of stories of men and women who heard the gospel and obeyed it. The eunuch on the road from Jerusalem to Gaza heard it and was baptized in the first body of water they came to (Acts 8:36-38). The Philippian jailer heard it and was baptized the same hour of the night (Acts 16:33). Saul of Tarsus heard it and was told to *"arise, and be baptized, and wash away thy sins, calling on the name of the Lord"* (Acts 22:16).

You do not have to wait to do this. You do not have to clean yourself up first. You do not have to figure out the lust before you come to the Lord. Christ is the one who breaks the lust. Christ is the one who gives the new heart. The renewing of the mind starts at the new birth. The new birth is something that happens to a sinner who hears the gospel, believes it, repents of his sins, confesses Christ, and is buried with him in baptism.

If that has never happened to you, do not turn another page of any book until that has happened to you. Find a faithful preacher. Find a church of Christ that teaches the Bible without apology. Tell someone you want to be baptized. Find me if need be. My information is all over the internet and social media. The whole rest of the Christian life flows out of that doorway. The watching, the deciding, the running, the renewing, the brighter light, all of them belong to the man and the woman who has been brought into the body of Christ. None of them works outside of him.

For the Christian, here is the final picture of the book.

The bug zapper is going to keep humming. The zappers of the world are not going away in your lifetime. The bait will keep being made by industries that have nothing to do with you personally and care nothing about your soul. The lust in you will keep showing up until the day you die, sometimes loudly, sometimes quietly, sometimes after years of quiet that make you think you had finally beaten it. There is no level of spiritual maturity in this life where the zapper stops humming. There is no nirvana.

What changes is where you live.

The Christian who has spent years being renewed by the Word, who has been in the assembly of the saints week after week, who has filled his hours with what is true and honest and just and pure and lovely, who has fled from what he should flee from and run toward what he should run toward, lives in a different kind of light than the man on the porch.

The moon, all this time, has been getting brighter to him.

The zapper has been getting dimmer.

The pull is still there. He can still feel it on certain nights. But he has somewhere brighter to be, and he knows where it is, and he goes there. The lust is no longer the brightest thing in his sky. He has been so flooded with the glory of God in the face of Jesus Christ that the bait has lost most of its dress. He sees the hook now. He sees the wires now. He has spent enough years in the moonlight that the porch light looks exactly what it is.

That is where this book is trying to take you. Not to a place of perfect mastery. Not to a place where you never get tempted again. To a place where the brighter light has become more real to you than the porch zapper, and the pull of lust has been outshone by the pull of the Lord.

There was a man who walked this whole road for you and did not fall.

He was tempted in the wilderness for forty days, and the bait was real, and the pull was real. The lust of an ordinary human stomach, an ordinary human pride, and an ordinary human ambition were tested in him to the limit of what any man could bear. He did not fall. He answered every piece of bait with the Word of God, and the bait did not catch.

He went to the cross with no sins of his own to pay for. He went to the cross because the rest of us had walked the road of sin all the way to its end, and the wage was due, and somebody had to pay it. He paid it. He died for sins he did not commit so that you and I could be forgiven for sins we did commit. He went into a tomb on a Friday afternoon and came out of it on a Sunday morning. He is alive forever, and he is the brighter light at the end of every fight you will ever fight.

> *"In him was life; and the life was the light of men. And the light shineth in darkness; and the darkness comprehended it not."* (John 1:4-5)

That light has been shining on you the whole time you have been reading this book. He is the brighter light. He is the only light strong enough to outshine the porch zapper. He is the one who has been waiting at the end of every road of sin you have walked, ready to forgive, ready to renew, ready to bring you home.

The June bug never knew about him. The June bug had no Christ. The June bug had no Bible, no assembly, no Word, no future, no hope. He flew at the only light he could see, and he died on the boards.

You are not the June bug.

You have a Bible. You have a Christ. You have a church. You have a Father who has been calling your name every evening of your life, like he called Adam's. You have a road back, and the road back is open right now.

Walk it.

For Discussion

1. Read 2 Corinthians 4:6. What does it mean that God has *shined in our hearts*? How does that change the way you fight against sin?

2. Read Romans 12:2. What is the difference between trying harder and *being transformed by the renewing of your mind*? Which one have you been doing?

3. Read Psalm 119:9-11. What is the role of the Word in cleansing a young man's way? How will you make the Word a daily part of your life from this point forward?

4. Read Hebrews 10:24-25. Why is the assembly of the saints not optional? What part of the brighter light is missing for the Christian who tries to walk this road alone?

5. Read Philippians 4:8. The mind will be filled with something. What in your life right now needs to be replaced by something on Paul's list?

6. If you have never been baptized into Christ, what is keeping you from doing it tonight? Read Acts 2:38. The road back is open. What is your next step?

7. Look back over the whole book. What are the three most important things you are taking with you out of this study? Write them down. Pray over them. Walk in them.

Thank You for Reading

Thank you for reading this book. I am grateful you gave it your time, and I pray it has been of help to you in some way.

I am always glad to hear from my readers. If you have a question, or if something in these pages stirred a thought you want to talk through, please reach out. I want to communicate with the people who read my work, and I will do my best to answer.

If this book helped you, I would ask one favor. Would you leave an honest five-star review on Amazon? It does more than you might think. A good review helps other people find the book, and it helps me keep writing and put solid material into more hands.

I would also invite you to visit my website at www.gagecoldwater.com. There you will find all of my books gathered in one place, along with many other resources. While you are there, you can sign up for my newsletter. That is the best way to know as soon as I release a new book or new content.

Thank you again for reading.

Gage Coldwater

Made in the USA
Coppell, TX
23 June 2026

83110070R00079